# NATURE SCHOOL:
# PLANET EARTH

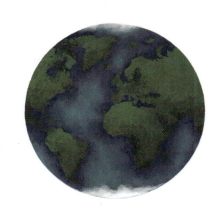

# NATURE SCHOOL:
# PLANET EARTH

### Lessons and Activities to Inspire Children's Fascination with Our Planet

Lauren Giordano
Stephanie Hathaway
Laura Stroup

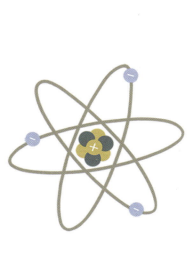

**Quarto.com**

© 2025 Quarto Publishing Group USA Inc.
Text and illustrations © 2025 Lauren Giordano, Stephanie Hathaway, Laura Stroup

First Published in 2025 by Quarry Books, an imprint of The Quarto Group,
100 Cummings Center, Suite 265-D, Beverly, MA 01915, USA.
T (978) 282-9590 F (978) 283-2742

All rights reserved. No part of this book may be reproduced in any form without written permission of the copyright owners. All images in this book have been reproduced with the knowledge and prior consent of the artists concerned, and no responsibility is accepted by producer, publisher, or printer for any infringement of copyright or otherwise, arising from the contents of this publication. Every effort has been made to ensure that credits accurately comply with information supplied. We apologize for any inaccuracies that may have occurred and will resolve inaccurate or missing information in a subsequent reprinting of the book.

Quarry Books titles are also available at discount for retail, wholesale, promotional, and bulk purchase. For details, contact the Special Sales Manager by email at specialsales@quarto.com or by mail at The Quarto Group, Attn: Special Sales Manager, 100 Cummings Center, Suite 265-D, Beverly, MA 01915, USA.

10 9 8 7 6 5 4 3 2 1

ISBN: 978-0-7603-9197-6

Digital edition published in 2025
eISBN: 978-0-7603-9198-3

Library of Congress Cataloging-in-Publication Data available

Design: Mattie Wells
Page Layout: Ashley Prine, Tandem Books
Illustration: Lauren Giordano, Stephanie Hathaway, Laura Stroup

Printed in China

## DEDICATION

This book is dedicated to all the stargazers and wave-chasers around the world. May we appreciate the intricacies of our planet, conserve Earth's natural resources, and understand our place in the global ecosystem.

# CONTENTS

Introduction - - - - - - - - - - - - - - 8

## 1 EARTH'S PLACE IN THE UNIVERSE

The Universe as We Know It - - - - - 12
Milky Way: Earth's Galactic Home - - - - - - - - - - - - - - - - - 14
Our Solar System - - - - - - - - - 16
The Planets - - - - - - - - - - - - 18
Earth and the Moon - - - - - - - 22
Celestial Influences - - - - - - - - 24
The Goldilocks Zone - - - - - - - 26
Earth's Natural History - - - - - - 28
Space Exploration - - - - - - - - - 30
Activities - - - - - - - - - - - - - - 32

## 2 EARTH'S COMPOSITION

Composition of Earth - - - - - - - 38
Magnetic Earth - - - - - - - - - - 40
Earth's Crust and Lithosphere - - - 42
Earth's Pedosphere - - - - - - - - 44
Plate Tectonics: Earth's Moving Parts - - - - - - - - - - - - 46
How Mountains Are Made - - - - 48
Earth's Geological Characteristics - 50
Earth's Natural Wonders - - - - - 52
Activities - - - - - - - - - - - - - - 56

## 3 EARTH'S HYDROSPHERE

| | |
|---|---|
| The Blue Planet | 62 |
| The Water Cycle | 64 |
| Properties of Water | 66 |
| Salt Water: Earth's Oceans | 68 |
| Seabed: The Landscape of the Ocean | 70 |
| Earth's Fresh Water | 72 |
| Earth's Groundwater | 74 |
| Earth's Cryosphere | 76 |
| How Water Shapes Earth | 78 |
| Activities | 80 |

## 5 LIFE ON EARTH

| | |
|---|---|
| Biosphere: Earth's Global Ecosystem | 112 |
| Ecology: The Interconnectedness of Life | 114 |
| Ecosystems | 116 |
| Ecosystems around the World | 118 |
| Location and Life on Earth | 122 |
| Energy Flow | 124 |
| Biodiversity: The Variety of Life | 126 |
| Life Cycles | 128 |
| Biochemical Cycles | 130 |
| Our Ever-Changing Earth | 132 |
| Activities | 134 |

## 4 EARTH'S ATMOSPHERE

| | |
|---|---|
| Composition of Earth's Atmosphere | 86 |
| Stratification: Layers of the Atmosphere | 88 |
| The Transfer of Heat Energy | 90 |
| Climate and Weather | 92 |
| Clouds | 94 |
| The Wild Wind | 96 |
| Types of Weather | 98 |
| What We See in the Sky | 102 |
| Air: Essential to Life on Earth | 104 |
| Activities | 106 |

| | |
|---|---|
| Acknowledgments | 138 |
| About the Authors | 139 |
| Index | 140 |

# INTRODUCTION

Our planet, our world, our home. *Planet Earth* reminds us just how incredible our little Goldilocks planet is. It investigates our place in the solar system and how we fit into the universe as a whole. As we study our world through the pages of this book, we gain not only knowledge but also understanding and appreciation for the little things and the big things that make our planet unique. And we look at Earth in a new light. From deep inside our rocky planet to the edges of its atmosphere, we explore the characteristics that make our world inhabitable and allow us to experience life here. And we discover the magnificence that is our planet: Earth.

## How to Use This Book

As you turn the pages of *Planet Earth*, we encourage you to read and ask questions. Make connections from the text with your own observations of things right outside your window, such as the night sky, soil, water cycles, and natural landforms. Earth is not a far-off, fairy-tale land. It is right under our feet everywhere we go, which makes *Planet Earth* a valuable tool for exploring the world. In this book, we have included chapters about Earth's place in the universe along with its physical composition, hydrosphere, atmosphere, and biosphere. Each chapter focuses on the different components that make Earth distinctive and habitable. You'll notice details about our solar system, Earth's layers, the power of water, weather, ecological communities, and much more. Hands-on activities accompany each chapter to reinforce your learning and to inspire outdoor adventures. We hope you enjoy the facts, figures, and fun in the pages of this book!

# Exploring Earth!

Our book is meant to encourage learning and exploration outdoors. As both parents and teachers, we appreciate acquiring knowledge, but we also seek practical ways to use this knowledge. Our bodies need to move and breathe fresh air. Research points to outdoor adventures like nature walks, hikes, and mindfulness as helping our attention spans, boosting our mental and physical health, and increasing our understanding of the natural world. So we made sure to include several ways to incorporate these fun and valuable nature experiences into your learning.

Exploring our planet can be as simple as immersing ourselves in the great outdoors. No special tools are necessary, but these supplies may support your nature observations and investigations:

- A nature journal, along with a pencil, encourages skills such as writing, noticing details, sketching, and more. And as you flip through your journals, you are reminded of the time you spent in nature and all the things you learned along the way.
- Pencils, colored pencils, and watercolors provide a way to record your adventures in real time or when you return home, remembering and reflecting on the events of the day.
- Both pocket microscopes and magnifying lenses allow you to get an up-close look at soil, rocks, and other items. They are easily transportable and can be used in the field or at home.
- Binoculars are designed to help you see flora, fauna, and even celestial bodies that are usually viewed from a distance. These may require some practice to use, and there are kid-size versions available.
- While not required, a telescope is an exciting way to view the Moon and other objects in the night sky.
- Small shovels for digging in the soil as well as containers for catching and observing creatures such as invertebrates come in handy.
- Identification books for animals and plant life native to your region are always helpful to have when you see a creature or plant you do not recognize.
- Water bottles and snacks are essential to bring along when out for the day.
- First-aid kits are useful in cases of scrapes and bumps on the trail. They come in all shapes and sizes, but we recommend something that will fit in your backpack.
- A comfortable and durable backpack can carry all your supplies while you're adventuring.

Thank you for picking up this book and exploring with us. We are truly passionate about family, nature, and education. Studying our home planet helps us have a deeper understanding of how things work and gives us endless opportunities to play, experiment, and learn. Reading about our place in the universe and Earth's composition prepares us to enjoy active discovery through hands-on experiences. *Planet Earth* is a book about our home, and it's applicable to all who peruse its pages. Earth has a story to tell, and we can't wait to share it with you.

INTRODUCTION

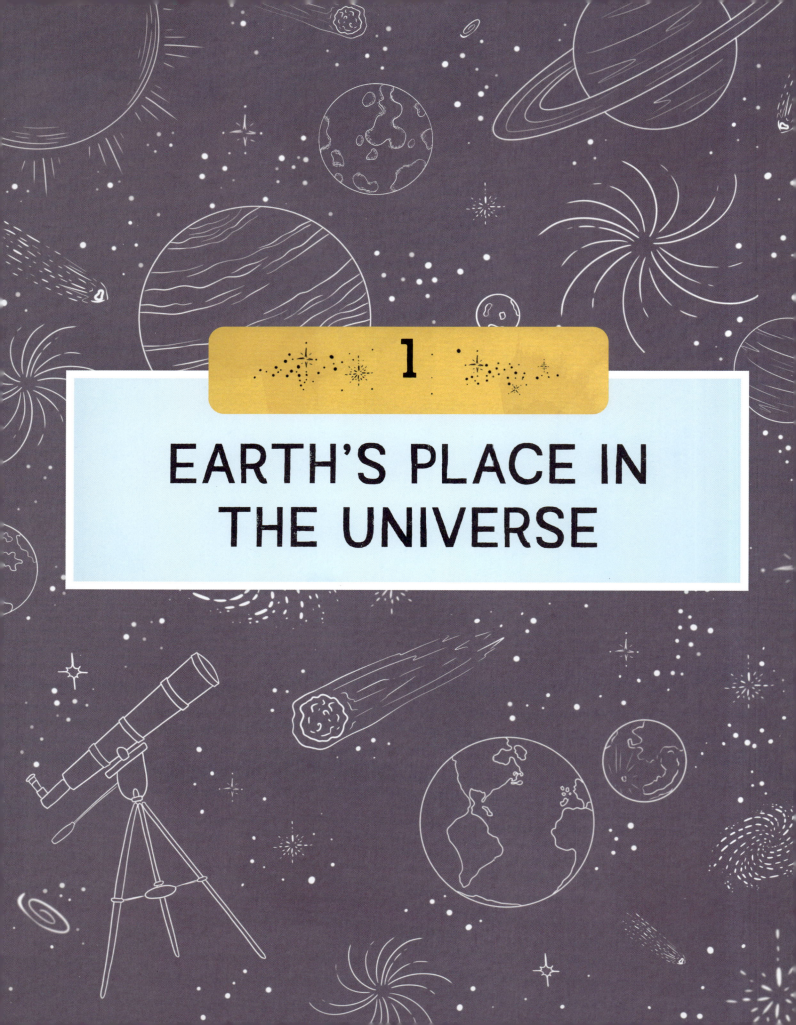

# 1

# EARTH'S PLACE IN THE UNIVERSE

From people's perspectives, Earth seems expansive. It feels like a huge planet for those living on it. In reality, Earth is a tiny cog in the machine that is the vast universe. In the Orion Spur of the Milky Way galaxy (just one of billions in the universe), Earth and seven other planets orbit a star called the Sun. This planetary system—or solar system, as we know it—is also home to moons, dwarf planets, asteroids, comets, and more, all held together by the force of gravity.

While Earth is not the largest planet in the solar system, it's the only one known to support life. As the third planet from the Sun, Earth is perfectly placed to experience bright days, dark nights, and a change of seasons each year. Both its orbit and its rotation contribute to Earth's unique biology. Patterns and rhythms such as migration, hibernation, and nesting experienced by living organisms all depend on Earth's relationship with the Sun.

Throughout this chapter, you will explore Earth's place in the cosmos, from its neighborhood in the solar system and the Milky Way to its small but important role in the boundless universe.

# THE UNIVERSE AS WE KNOW IT

What makes up the universe? To put it simply . . . everything! Earth is just a small part of the universe, and even though the solar system and galaxy may seem gigantic, they are just a tiny fraction of the universe in its entirety. Earth and the Moon, along with all the other planets, moons, stars, comets, asteroids, matter, and energy, combine to make up the universe.

## Observable Universe

Because of the sheer vastness of the whole universe, we are not able to see and study it entirely. Scientists refer to the parts we have been able to detect from Earth over the ages as "the observable universe." Scientists believe the universe may be without physical borders or boundaries. Based on the fact that light is needed to see, along with the proposed age of Earth and the theory of a continually expanding universe, scientists estimate the diameter of the **observable universe** to be over 90 billion light-years. While Earth isn't at the center of the whole universe, it is at the center of the observable universe, because that is measured from our planet's perspective.

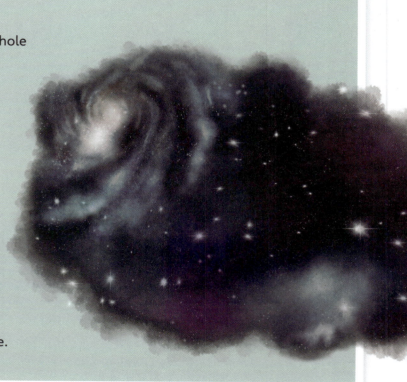

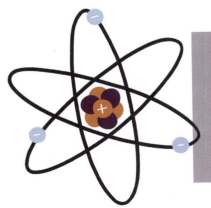

### FUN FACT

Microscopic particles called atoms, which contain protons, neutrons, and electrons, make up all matter in the universe. Protons are positively charged, while electrons are negative. Neutrons have no charge at all.

NATURE SCHOOL: PLANET EARTH

## Interstellar and Intergalactic Space

Interstellar space is simply the space between stars. This space begins beyond the far reaches of the Sun's heliosphere, extending past the planets in our solar system. Containing mostly gas and dust, the particles in interstellar space are spread apart. Intergalactic space, or the space between galaxies, may span millions of light-years from one galaxy to the next.

### FUN FACT
Black holes are often formed when a large star explodes and collapses, creating such an incredible density that not even light can escape its gravitational pull.

## History of Space Study

Throughout history, cultures and civilizations have gazed at the cosmos and tried to explain what they observed. Changes in the Moon's shape as well as constellations and eclipses prompted stories and early studies of astronomy. Ancient astronomers created calendars and constructed structures to view the sky. The Babylonians are often credited as being the first to record their astronomical studies around 750 BCE. Ancient Chinese astronomers created stellar catalogs and recorded solar eclipses. Ancient Greeks applied mathematics to measure distances of celestial bodies and their orbits, and they proposed that Earth is spherical rather than flat.

EARTH'S PLACE IN THE UNIVERSE

# MILKY WAY: EARTH'S GALACTIC HOME

The Milky Way is the "neighborhood" where Earth dwells in the universe. The Milky Way is believed to be a spiral galaxy possessing two major arms thick with stars and extending from the galaxy's central bar.

### FUN FACT

You may know that Earth and the other planets in the solar system orbit the Sun, but did you know that the solar system orbits the center of the Milky Way? While it takes a year for Earth to make one revolution around the Sun, it will take the solar system over 200 million years to travel around the galactic center! And it's moving at quite a clip—over 500,000 miles (804,000 km) per hour!

NATURE SCHOOL: PLANET EARTH

## Anatomy of the Milky Way

A combination of dust, gas, and stars, this galaxy measures close to 100,000 light-years wide. If you were to see the Milky Way's profile view, it may look like a flat disk, with the central bar bulging out in the middle. The Sun and the solar system are located in the Orion Spur of the Milky Way, midway between the central bar and the edge of the galaxy. Scientists estimate there are hundreds of billions of stars in the Milky Way.

- The barred, spiral galaxy where Earth and the solar system are located is called the **Milky Way**.
- The star at the center of the solar system is called the **Sun**. Earth and the other planets revolve, or orbit, around it.
- Dense, spherical groups of older, red stars held together by a strong gravitational pull are known as **globular clusters**.
- The main structure of the spiral galaxy of the Milky Way is a rotating, star-filled **galactic disk**. The disk shape forms from the galaxy's rotation.
- The **stellar halo** surrounds the Milky Way as a football-shaped cloud of stars.

### The Milky Way in the Night Sky

It is possible to see parts of the Milky Way in the night sky, especially when in rural locations, far away from city lights. Not surprisingly, it has a dull, milky-white appearance. Of all the stars in the galaxy, only a few thousand are visible from Earth with the naked eye. While the name "Milky Way" stems from Greek mythology and Hera spilling milk into the sky, different cultures around the world have other names for the galaxy, including "Silver River" and "Path of the Birds."

EARTH'S PLACE IN THE UNIVERSE

# OUR SOLAR SYSTEM

The solar system is Earth's galactic neighborhood. It contains the Sun and all the planets, asteroids, comets, gas, dust, and other celestial objects. Vastly spread out with great distances between them, the planets orbit the Sun due to its powerful gravitational pull.

## The Sun

The Sun holds special importance for Earth, as its light and heat allow life to flourish. The Sun is considered a medium-size star, with a diameter of 1.4 million kilometers. Made up of mostly hydrogen and helium, its intense heat means these elements are in a plasma state. The Sun's hot **core** reaches temperatures greater than 27 million degrees Fahrenheit (15 million degrees C) and radiates light and heat. This energy travels through the Sun's **radiative zone.** Then, the **convective zone** transfers the energy by waves of convection. Its plasma heats up, spreads out, and moves toward the **photosphere** before cooling, becoming dense, and sinking back down.

Several solar features have been observed while studying the Sun.

- CORONA—the Sun's hot, atmospheric outer layer, extending millions of miles from its surface
- CORONAL LOOPS—hot plasma that flows along the Sun's magnetic field, extending high above the Sun's surface
- SOLAR PROMINENCE—plasma arches emanating from the Sun's surface
- CHROMOSPHERE—a colorful layer of the Sun's lower atmosphere where hydrogen emits reddish light

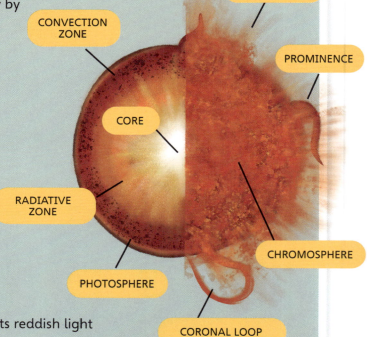

### FUN FACT

Solar wind from the Sun's corona can travel over 1 million miles (1.6 million km) per hour through space. This plasma, made mostly of charged particles, usually travels around Earth thanks to its magnetosphere.

NATURE SCHOOL: PLANET EARTH

## The Inner Solar System

Earth along with the other terrestrial planets and the asteroid belt make up the inner solar system. The solid planets in the inner solar system have hard surfaces and may have other features, such as mountains, valleys, and craters. Nearest to the Sun is Mercury, followed by Venus, then Earth and Mars. Past Mars lies the asteroid belt that contains not only asteroids but also the inner solar system's only dwarf planet, Ceres.

## Outer Solar System

The outer solar system is where the gas giants are found. Also known as Jovian planets, Jupiter, Saturn, Uranus, and Neptune are composed mostly of gas. Far beyond Neptune exists a cold region known as the Kuiper Belt, which is believed to contain icy space objects with not only water ice but frozen gases as well. Centaurs, small, icy bodies believed to originate in the Kuiper Belt, orbit around the Sun between Jupiter and Neptune.

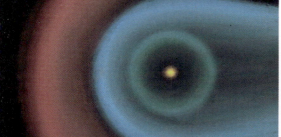

### FUN FACT

The outer edge of the solar system is often called the heliopause. This boundary marks where the farthest reaches of the Sun's solar wind meets interstellar space.

EARTH'S PLACE IN THE UNIVERSE

# THE PLANETS

Earth is one of eight major planets in the solar system. All the planets revolve around, or orbit, the Sun. Some of these planets have rings, and many have their own moons. Together with the Sun, asteroids, and comets, they make up our celestial neighborhood.

Mercury is both the closest planet to the Sun and the smallest planet in the solar system. It orbits the Sun quickly, making one revolution in just 88 Earth days.

Venus is described as the hottest planet in the solar system due to the heat trapped by its dense atmosphere. Venus is close in size to Earth and is often referred to as Earth's twin.

With a diameter of approximately 8,000 miles (12,900 km), Earth is the fifth-largest planet in the solar system. It takes Earth 365 days to orbit the Sun, which is equal to one Earth year.

Mars glows red in the night sky. Mars is known as the red planet and appears that color because of oxidized iron on its surface and dust in its atmosphere.

NATURE SCHOOL: PLANET EARTH

The largest planet in the solar system, Jupiter is more massive than all the other planets combined. Jupiter's name comes from the king of the gods in Roman mythology.

Saturn is well-known for its icy rings, which stretch outward 175,000 miles (281,600 km) from its surface. Saturn rotates on a tilted axis similar to Earth and experiences seasons due to its tilt.

Methane gas gives Uranus its blue-green hue. This planet has two sets of rings surrounding it. Uranus spins on its side and looks like it is rolling along as it orbits the Sun.

Neptune is 2.8 billion (4.5 billion km) miles from the Sun, which is the farthest of any planet in the solar system. Before the planet was discovered, mathematical calculations allowed scientists to predict its location.

### FUN FACT

Once the solar system's ninth planet, Pluto was reclassified as a dwarf planet in 2006. Pluto is located in the Kuiper Belt, a great distance from the Sun.

EARTH'S PLACE IN THE UNIVERSE

19

# EARTH'S ORBIT AND ROTATION

Earth is positioned approximately 93 million (149 million km) miles away from the Sun. Since its orbit is shaped like an ellipse, similar to an oval or flattened circle, Earth is not always the same distance from the Sun. It reaches its perihelion, its closest distance, in early January. It reaches its aphelion, or farthest distance, in early July. As Earth moves around the Sun, it completes one revolution every 365.25 days. Earth travels over 580 million miles (933 million km) while it follows its orbital path and reaches speeds of 67,000 miles (108,000 km) per hour. While speeding around the Sun, Earth is also spinning over 1,000 miles (1,600 km) per hour near its equator!

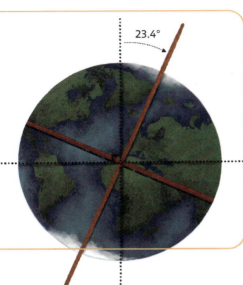

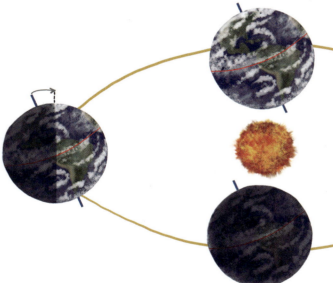

SPRING (Northern Hemisphere)
AUTUMN (Southern Hemisphere)

WINTER (Northern Hemisphere)
SUMMER (Southern Hemisphere)

SUMMER (Northern Hemisphere)
WINTER (Southern Hemisphere)

AUTUMN (Northern Hemisphere)
SPRING (Southern Hemisphere)

## Axial Tilt and the Seasons

Earth rotates along an imaginary axis, which is tilted at a 23.4-degree angle. Earth's tilt can vary slightly, and it's this tilt that allows Earth to experience seasons. When the Northern Hemisphere is angled toward the Sun, it experiences more direct sunlight, resulting in warmer temperatures. The same result occurs in the Southern Hemisphere when it is tilted toward the Sun. The hemisphere tilted away from the Sun experiences colder temperatures.

### FUN FACT

Since Earth's trip around the Sun takes 365.25 days, an extra day is added to the calendar every four years in February. This is known as a leap year.

NATURE SCHOOL: PLANET EARTH

# Day and Night

In addition to revolving around the Sun, Earth spins, or rotates, on its axis. One rotation takes 24 hours. As Earth rotates, different areas of the planet face the Sun and experience daytime. The side of Earth turned away from the Sun experiences night. A daily rhythm of events that occurs every 24 hours is known as a diurnal cycle.

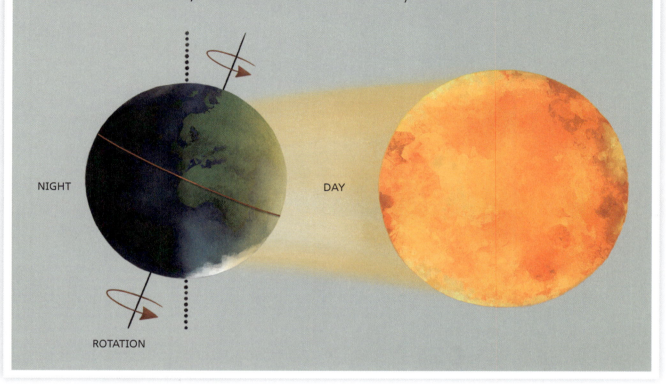

NIGHT  DAY

ROTATION

## MIDNIGHT SUN

There are places on Earth in the regions of the Arctic and Antarctic Circles where the Sun never sets below the horizon during the summer months. This natural phenomenon is known as the "midnight sun."

# EARTH AND THE MOON

Known as "luna" in Latin, the Moon is the biggest and brightest celestial object visible from Earth. As Earth's only natural satellite, the Moon orbits our planet once every 27 days. Besides providing light, affecting the ocean tides, and influencing wildlife navigation and behavior in different species, scientists believe the Moon's gravitational pull helps Earth remain tilted at a constant angle.

While the entire Moon is always in the night sky and doesn't change, its appearance varies throughout the month depending on how much of the Moon is illuminated by sunlight. During the new-moon phase, the side of the Moon facing Earth is in darkness, so the Moon is not visible. It takes approximately 29 days for the Moon to go through all its phases, resulting in one lunar month. This takes slightly longer than the 27 days the Moon takes to revolve around Earth, because as the Moon is orbiting Earth, they are both orbiting the Sun.

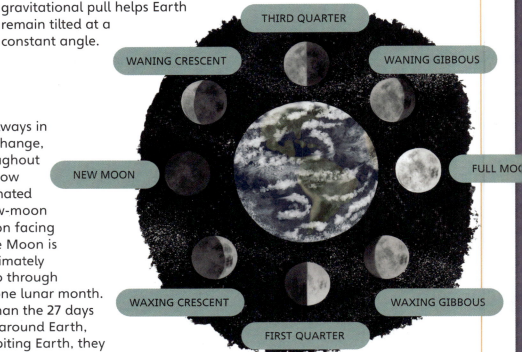

## FUN FACT

The Moon travels nearly 1.5 million miles (2.4 million km) each time it orbits Earth. During its revolution, the Moon is also rotating at the same rate, resulting in a **synchronous rotation**. This means that people on Earth see only one side of the Moon. This visible side is known as the near side, while the other side is called the far side.

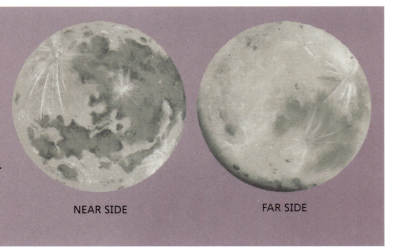

NEAR SIDE     FAR SIDE

NATURE SCHOOL: PLANET EARTH
22

# The Tides

Tides occur where water from the ocean meets the coast. High and low tides are primarily caused by the Moon's gravitational pull on both Earth and the water on it. High tides will occur on the side of Earth closest to the Moon and the side of Earth opposite the Moon, while low tides occur on the sides of our planet that are perpendicular to the Moon's position. When the Sun, the Moon, and Earth are aligned, tides are higher than normal, resulting in a spring tide. Neap tides are lower than normal, and they occur when the Moon and Sun form a right angle in relation to Earth.

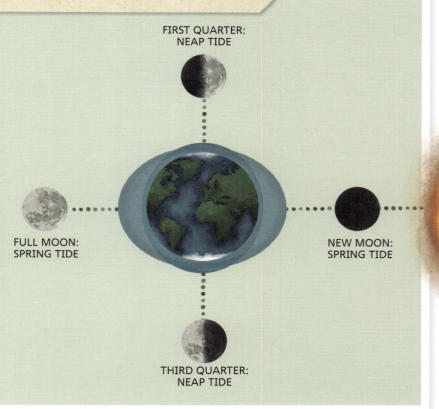

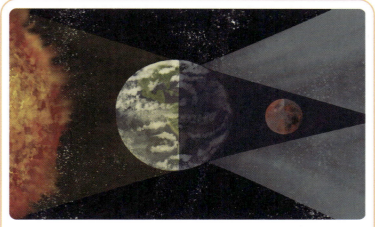

## Eclipses

A few times each year, the Sun, Earth, and the Moon align. As the Moon travels through the shadow cast by Earth when Earth is between the Sun and the Moon, an eclipse occurs. During a lunar eclipse, the Moon appears to be a reddish color due to the scattering of blue light waves from the Sun as they travel through Earth's atmosphere.

### FUN FACT

The Moon may be Earth's only natural satellite, but over 9,000 human-made satellites orbit Earth to do things such as provide internet and phone service, gather weather data, and allow global positioning for GPS services.

EARTH'S PLACE IN THE UNIVERSE

# CELESTIAL INFLUENCES

Earth shares space in the solar system with other planets, moons, asteroids, comets, and space debris. These celestial objects can come into contact with Earth and its atmosphere, having the potential to influence Earth's geology and life both on land and in the sea. And the gravitational pull from the Sun, the Moon, and even large planets like Jupiter and Saturn affect Earth's tilt and orbit.

ASTEROID

METEOR

COMET

## Asteroids, Meteors, and Comets

**Asteroids** are rocky objects that orbit the Sun, mainly in the asteroid belt between Mars and Jupiter. Usually chunks of rock and metal from comets and asteroids, **meteors** burn bright when they make their way through Earth's atmosphere. **Comets** are often found at the outskirts of the solar system and are made from dust and ice. They have a frozen nucleus at their center and long tails of gases trailing behind. As they orbit the Sun, comets are occasionally visible from Earth.

### FUN FACT

Left behind after a huge meteorite slammed into Earth thousands of years ago, Meteor Crater is found outside of Flagstaff, Arizona, in the United States. This colossal crater spans nearly 1 mile (1.6 km) across and is 550 feet (168 m) deep.

NATURE SCHOOL: PLANET EARTH

## Ancient Impacts

The impact of a giant asteroid colliding with Earth is credited with causing the mass extinction of many species, including large dinosaurs. Scientists estimate this collision took place as the Mesozoic Era ended, nearly 66 million years ago. The Chicxulub crater, near the Yucatán Peninsula in Mexico, marks the spot where the asteroid struck Earth.

### FUN FACT

In 1908, an apparent asteroid exploded in the sky above a remote section of Siberia in Russia. In an explosion known as the Tunguska event, the asteroid broke apart approximately 6 miles (10 km) above Earth's surface, resulting in shock waves, fires, and heat felt for miles.

## Shooting Stars

Seen from Earth, shooting stars look like stars moving across the sky and vanishing. But they're not actually stars. Rather, they are meteors that burn up as they fly through Earth's atmosphere, leaving a trail of light as they vaporize. Sometimes, many meteors stream through the atmosphere, creating what are known as meteor showers.

EARTH'S PLACE IN THE UNIVERSE

# THE GOLDILOCKS ZONE

While scientists have found "hints" that life may exist elsewhere in the universe, it has yet to actually be found. Planets with compositions similar to Earth, along with evidence of water and carbon, lead scientists to hypothesize that life may be found in other areas of our solar system and beyond.

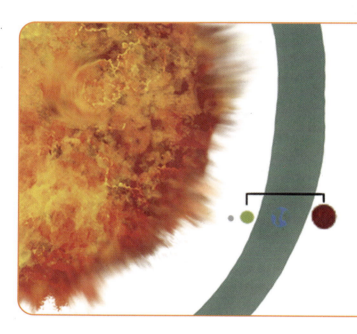

## Habitable Zone

The habitable zone describes a planet with the right conditions for life, especially a planet that is not too close to or too far from its star. The temperature of a planet in the habitable zone allows water to exist in its liquid form. Often, this zone of habitability is referred to as the **Goldilocks zone** because conditions are "just right" for life, similar to those on Earth.

## Planetary Habitability

Habitability is not solely determined by a planet's distance from a star, and water is not the only requirement for life. Scientists tend to look for conditions similar to those on Earth, such as adequate light for photosynthesis along with components for nutrients and energy. Carbon, nitrogen, and oxygen are important resources in this category. Scientists also consider the type of radiation given off by its star along with a planet's protective atmosphere to be important factors.

NATURE SCHOOL: PLANET EARTH

## Ingredients for Life

Several factors make life on Earth possible. Besides being the perfect distance from the Sun to keep temperatures livable, Earth receives light and heat from the **Sun** to power photosynthesis and keep Earth from freezing. **Water** and **elements** such as carbon and nitrogen supply ecosystems with important resources, while the atmosphere both insulates Earth and protects it from harmful radiation from the Sun.

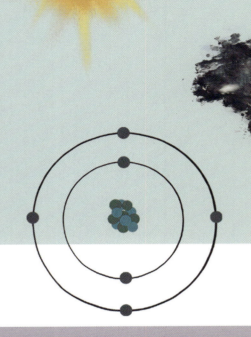

## Other Stars with Potential

While Earth's solar system has only one planet in a habitable zone, scientists estimate other stars may have up to seven potentially habitable planets around them. Many factors influence this number, such as the size and brightness of the star as well the shape of the planets' orbits.

### FUN FACT

Rovers, vehicles designed to traverse rocky planets, have collected samples and images on Mars that lead scientists to believe rivers and lakes once existed on that planet.

EARTH'S PLACE IN THE UNIVERSE

# EARTH'S NATURAL HISTORY

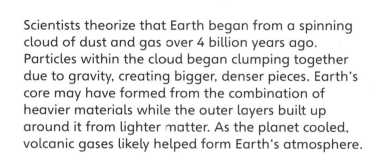

Scientists theorize that Earth began from a spinning cloud of dust and gas over 4 billion years ago. Particles within the cloud began clumping together due to gravity, creating bigger, denser pieces. Earth's core may have formed from the combination of heavier materials while the outer layers built up around it from lighter matter. As the planet cooled, volcanic gases likely helped form Earth's atmosphere.

## Formation of a Planetary System

In order for planetary systems, like the solar system, to form around a **star**, **dust particles** with elements such as carbon and iron are important building blocks. Found in the **gaseous disk** around a newly formed star, these particles crash together and eventually create large chunks of rock known as **planetesimals** that orbit the star. Scientists theorize that colder areas, far from the central star, allow gas and ice to form planets farther away. And terrestrial planets are more likely to form in the warmer regions closer to the star.

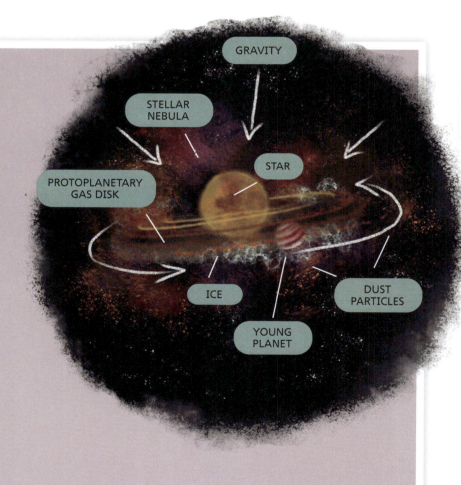

NATURE SCHOOL: PLANET EARTH

## The Life and Death of a Star

Similar to all living things, stars are born, grow and develop, and then die. All types of stars form from a cloud of gas known as a **solar nebula**. A yellow dwarf star like the Sun is thought to have an average life span of 10 billion years.

1. As gas particles collide, their gravity increases, and they begin to spin, causing a rise in temperature and the formation of a **protostar**.
2. When enough heat builds up for hydrogen gases to fuse into helium, the star will brighten and enter its **main sequence** phase, like the Sun is in currently.
3. Eventually, a star will run out of fuel in its core, causing it to cool and contract. The outer layer of the star pushes outward and becomes a **red giant** named for its glowing red color.
4. The Sun and other stars of similar mass will collapse and end their life cycle as white dwarf stars and then **black dwarfs**.

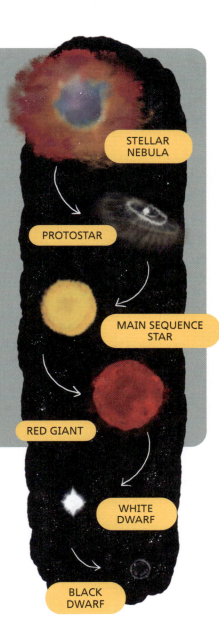

STELLAR NEBULA
PROTOSTAR
MAIN SEQUENCE STAR
RED GIANT
WHITE DWARF
BLACK DWARF

## Geological Time

We use days, weeks, and months to measure time with a calendar, but the geological time scale is much more epic in nature. From the largest sections—which range from eons to shorter eras, periods, epochs, and ages—the geological time scale measures much larger chunks of time from thousands to millions and billions of years. These measurements often mark the appearance or extinction of groups of living things throughout Earth's history.

| PRECAMBRIAN | | | | | | PHANEROZOIC | | | | | | | | | | | EON |
|---|---|---|---|---|---|---|---|---|---|---|---|---|---|---|---|---|---|
| ARCHEAN | | | PROTEROZOIC | | | PALEOZOIC | | | | | | MESOZOIC | | | CENOZOIC | | ERA |
| HADEAN | EOARCHEAN | PALEOARCHEAN | MESOARCHEAN | NEOARCHEAN | PALEOPROTEROZOIC | MESOPROTEROZOIC | NEOPROTEROZOIC | CAMBRIAN | ORDOVICIAN | SILURIAN | DEVONIAN | CARBONIFEROUS | PERMIAN | TRIASSIC | JURASSIC | CRETACEOUS | PALEOGENE | NEOGENE | QUATERNARY | PERIOD |

EARTH'S PLACE IN THE UNIVERSE

# SPACE EXPLORATION

Humans have always been intrigued by the sky and its celestial objects. And humans have found ways to study and explore these things dating back to ancient times. People have used watchtowers to observe the sky and map the stars, kept records of cosmic events, and used mathematics to calculate sizes of space objects and the distances between them. In the 1600s, famous Italian scientist Galileo Galilei built a rudimentary telescope to view the sky. He discovered physical features of the Moon's surface, as well as moons orbiting Jupiter. His observations of Venus led him to believe the planets orbited the Sun, a controversial claim at the time.

GALILEO GALILEI

## What Is Astronomy?

The study of celestial objects and the universe surrounding them beyond Earth's atmosphere is known as astronomy. Ancient astronomers saw the same things we see today, without the help of a telescope or other modern exploration tools.

### FUN FACT

Launched in 1990, the Hubble Space Telescope orbits 320 miles (515 km) above Earth and doesn't have interference from Earth's atmosphere, light pollution, or weather. Hubble is able to gather clearer images than telescopes on the ground, and it is serviceable by astronauts in its low-Earth orbit.

NATURE SCHOOL: PLANET EARTH

## Humans in Space

Humans first entered space in 1961 when Yuri Gagarin, a Soviet cosmonaut, orbited Earth a single time. In 1965, another cosmonaut performed the first spacewalk while tethered to his space capsule. In 1969, the United States landed on the Moon, and Neil Armstrong was the first human to walk on the Moon's surface.

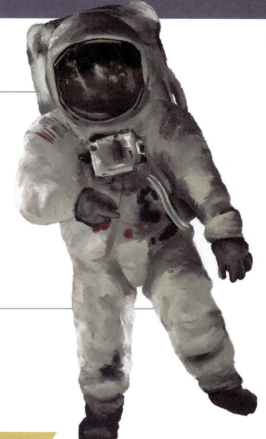

### FUN FACT

The International Space Station (ISS), a collaborative effort between 15 countries, hosted its first crew in the year 2000 after several years of construction both on Earth and in space. The ISS orbits Earth approximately 250 miles (402 km) from the planet's surface, acting as a research laboratory that is expected to function through 2030.

## Why Explore Space?

Human curiosity may have initiated space exploration, but the hope of visiting new worlds and expanding technology inspires people to continue. Exploring space yields information about the solar system, galaxy, and universe. And potentially, it may reveal clues to the origin of the cosmos.

EARTH'S PLACE IN THE UNIVERSE

# ACTIVITIES

In chapter one, you explored Earth's place in the universe and discovered the unique characteristics of our planet that make it habitable for living things. You learned about the celestial bodies nearest Earth and were introduced to the different ways humans have surveyed the heavens since ancient times. Now, it's your turn to study Earth's solar system "neighborhood" with these hands-on activities.

## Nature Journal

Do you have a favorite planet? Choose one of the planets in the solar system to explore in more depth. Make a nature journal entry, complete with an accurate illustration of the planet you chose. Be sure to include information such as the planet's name, where it is located in the solar system, its size and composition, its distance from the Sun, whether it has rings and/or moons, and any other facts you find interesting.

## Build a Solar System Model

Discover more about the planets and other celestial bodies in the solar system as you construct a model of the solar system. Use salt dough, or purchase foam balls of different sizes to use for the Sun and planets. Carefully research the characteristics of each to demonstrate size differences of the various space objects, even if they are not completely to scale. Draw the planets' orbits with white marker or colored pencil around the Sun, and then arrange the planets in the correct order. Be sure to label each planet. Alternatively, the Sun can be at one end of the model with the planets next to the Sun in order from closest to farthest away.

# Sunography

Use the power of the Sun to make special solar art prints, also known as cyanotypes. This works best on a sunny day, but sunlight also reaches Earth on cloudy days. The paper will just need to sit for several minutes in the Sun.

1. Gather your supplies: sun print paper (found at craft stores or online); a clipboard or tray; a shallow pan or tray with water; relatively flat nature items such as leaves, flowers, and grasses; and a flat surface outside on which to set everything.
2. Plan out a pattern you would like to make on the paper with your nature items.
3. Place the shallow pan with water in the shade next to your work area. Set out your paper, bluish side up, on a clipboard or tray in a shaded area out of direct sunlight, and arrange the nature items in your preferred pattern.
4. Move the clipboard or tray to direct sunlight, and let your creation soak up the Sun for a couple of minutes, until the bluish color of the paper turns white. *If it's breezy, you can set a sheet of clear acrylic over your nature items, so they don't blow around.
5. Take your paper back to the shaded work area, and remove the nature items from your paper. Submerge the paper in the tray of water, and rinse it until the pattern appears (approximately 2 minutes). The image will be white while the rest of the paper turns blue.
6. Set out the paper on a towel to dry thoroughly, or hang it up with clothespins. Then frame your solar print, use it as wrapping paper, or make a notecard with it.

EARTH'S PLACE IN THE UNIVERSE

# ACTIVITIES

## Night-Sky Painting

For this project, you will need a piece of white watercolor paper, crayons, watercolor paints and a brush, and a cup of water. First, using your crayons, press hard to create stars, the moon, a comet, or whatever night-sky features you would like to add to your watercolor paper. You can also include your house below the sky, or a landscape or cityscape along the bottom of the paper. Then, using a mix of dark-blue and black watercolors, paint over your crayon drawings on the paper. The paint will not stick to the waxy crayon, but it will fill in the spaces in between to portray a dark sky around the shining cosmic features you created.

## Night Hike

Hiking during the day is fun, but night hikes can be just as exciting. And hiking at night allows you to see something that is often difficult to see during the day—the Moon! The Moon does not give off its own light, but the Sun's light reflects off the Moon's rocky surface, making it visible at night. Take your nature journal, a pencil, a flashlight, and binoculars with you for your hike. If possible, hike away from the bright lights of the city, and be sure to hike in a safe, familiar location. You can even use your own backyard. When first viewing the Moon, use just your eyes. Can you distinguish the light areas from the darker craters? Sketch what you see. Then, try using the binoculars to view the Moon. Can you see anything that wasn't visible with just your eyes? Add those new details to your sketch.

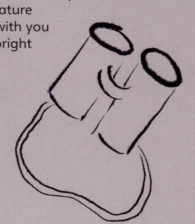

NATURE SCHOOL: PLANET EARTH

## Film Canister Rocket

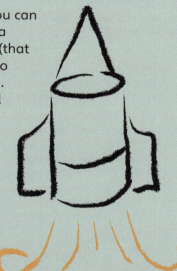

You can make your own model rocket using a film canister, which you can likely pick up at your local camera store, or a similar container with a snap-on lid that can easily pop off. You'll also need antacid tablets (that fizz in water) and water. You may also want cardstock and scissors to cut out fins for your rocket and markers to decorate it before launch. An outdoor space with a level surface for launching your rocket and protective eyewear are also important.

1. Launching your rocket is quite simple. Just fill your canister approximately two-thirds full with water.
2. Then, when you're outdoors in your launch space, put on your safety goggles, drop an antacid tablet into the water in the canister, quickly put on the lid, and set it UPSIDE DOWN on the ground.
3. The antacid tablet and water will create carbon dioxide gas that increases the pressure inside the canister. Eventually, the pressure will be high enough to pop the canister off the lid and up into the air!

## Did You Know?

Earth is considered to be 1 astronomical unit (au) from the Sun, which is equivalent to approximately 150 million kilometers. In comparison, the closest planet to the Sun is Mercury, which is 0.39 au. The farthest planet from the Sun in our solar system is Neptune, at over 30 au.

*Planet Distance from Sun (au)*

Mercury 0.39     Jupiter 5.2

Venus 0.72       Saturn 9.54

Earth 1          Uranus 19.2

Mars 1.52        Neptune 30.06

EARTH'S PLACE IN THE UNIVERSE

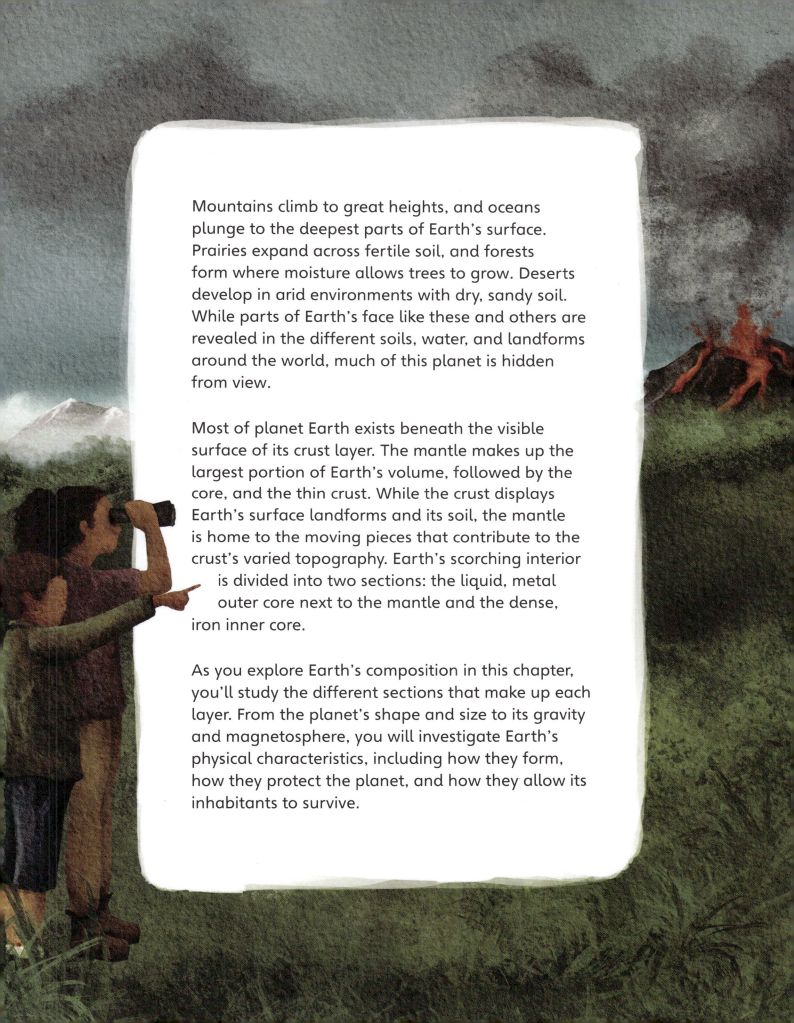

Mountains climb to great heights, and oceans plunge to the deepest parts of Earth's surface. Prairies expand across fertile soil, and forests form where moisture allows trees to grow. Deserts develop in arid environments with dry, sandy soil. While parts of Earth's face like these and others are revealed in the different soils, water, and landforms around the world, much of this planet is hidden from view.

Most of planet Earth exists beneath the visible surface of its crust layer. The mantle makes up the largest portion of Earth's volume, followed by the core, and the thin crust. While the crust displays Earth's surface landforms and its soil, the mantle is home to the moving pieces that contribute to the crust's varied topography. Earth's scorching interior is divided into two sections: the liquid, metal outer core next to the mantle and the dense, iron inner core.

As you explore Earth's composition in this chapter, you'll study the different sections that make up each layer. From the planet's shape and size to its gravity and magnetosphere, you will investigate Earth's physical characteristics, including how they form, how they protect the planet, and how they allow its inhabitants to survive.

# COMPOSITION OF EARTH

Divided into different layers, Earth has a crust, mantle, and core. The central **core** has both a solid inner section and liquid outer section. The continental and oceanic **crusts** are more visible on the outer surface of Earth than the layers inside, but they only account for 1 percent of the planet's volume. The **mantle** makes up most of Earth's volume at approximately 84 percent while the core accounts for 15 percent.

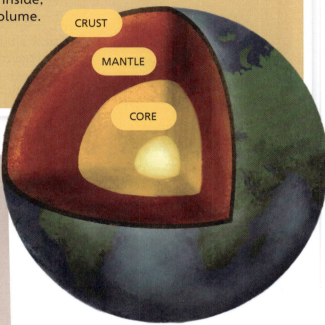

## FUN FACT

Earth's core is extremely hot, which scientists theorize is due to both the heat from collisions during Earth's formation and the heat generated from decaying radioactive elements in its core. While this heat doesn't greatly impact the temperature felt on Earth's surface, it does contribute to the movement of Earth's plates, which causes earthquakes and volcanic eruptions and changes the planet's topography.

## Size and Shape of Earth

Earth has a reputation for being round, and it appears that way when viewed from space. However, Earth is actually an oblate spheroid, and an ever-changing one at that. Earth is nearly a sphere, but it bulges around the equator due to the centrifugal force created by its rotation. Earth's diameter is actually shorter from the North Pole to the South Pole than it is when measured across the equator. From pole to pole, the diameter is approximately 7,900 miles (12,700 km); along the equator, it is 7,926 miles (12,755 km) across. Keep in mind, Earth changes shape regularly with tidal pulls on both Earth's water and crust. And the movement of Earth's crust from earthquakes and volcanic eruptions also changes its shape.

NATURE SCHOOL: PLANET EARTH

# Earth's Layers

Earth's outermost layer is the crust. **Continental crust** covers approximately 41 percent of the planet, and **oceanic crust** surrounds the rest. Made from rocks and minerals, the solid crust forms Earth's topography, from magnificent mountains to pleasant plains.

The **mantle** forms the largest of Earth's layers, made mostly of silicates—minerals that contain silicon and oxygen. Pressure and temperature increase deep within Earth's mantle. Much of the mantle contains solid materials, but at plate boundaries, rock may be more "plastic" or flexible.

The **outer core** is made of iron and nickel that is mostly liquid, which means it has low viscosity. As this metal moves around in the outer core, electrical currents in the liquid metal contribute to Earth's magnetic field. The **inner core**, made up of mostly iron, is full of heat and pressure, which keeps the iron in a solid form.

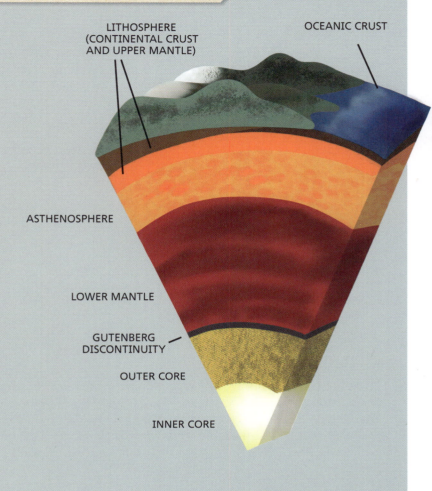

## FUN FACT

Ancient Greek philosopher Aristotle studied many disciplines, including biology, chemistry, and physics. He was one of the first people to propose Earth's roundness based on observations. He reasoned that because the visibility of constellations changes with latitude and Earth's shadow appears round during a lunar eclipse, Earth must be round in shape.

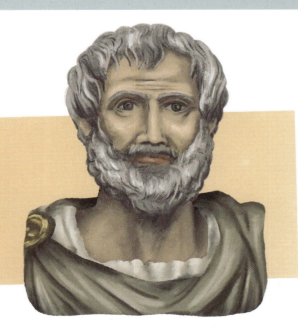

EARTH'S COMPOSITION

# MAGNETIC EARTH

## Earth's Dynamic Core

Journey to the center of Earth, and you'll find the viscous liquid outer core and solid inner core beyond that. While the inner core is hot enough to melt the metal from which it's made, persistent pressure deep inside Earth keeps it solid.

## Earth's Magnetosphere

Earth's magnetic field, known as the **magnetosphere**, is generated near Earth's center. The liquid outer core creates and conducts electrical currents that power the magnetosphere in what some scientists theorize is a self-sustaining "geodynamo." Earth's rotation and Coriolis forces keep the liquid metal in the outer core moving in spirals and working together to power Earth's magnetic field. The movement of the liquid in the outer core can vary the location of Earth's **magnetic poles** each year.

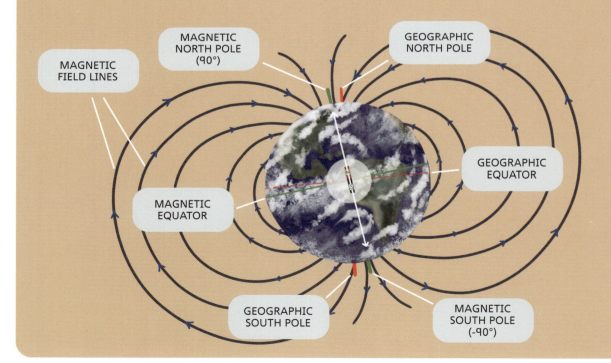

NATURE SCHOOL: PLANET EARTH

## EARTH'S PROTECTIVE SHIELD

The magnetosphere surrounds and protects Earth from harmful cosmic rays and damaging radiation clouds from the Sun. It deflects dangerous particles and keeps them from reaching the planet. However, some of the solar energy does make it through in what's known as "space weather."

### FUN FACT

Unlike Earth's thunderstorms with rain, wind, and lightning, geomagnetic storms occur when large numbers of solar particles and energy are sent into space from the Sun. They are more common during times of high solar activity. Geomagnetic storms can cause issues with power grids, radio waves, and satellites.

### FUN FACT

What goes up must come down, right? That's because of **gravity**, the force of attraction drawing objects together. Earth's mass is what keeps things falling down, as they are attracted toward Earth's center rather than up toward the sky.

## EARTH'S COMPOSITION

# EARTH'S CRUST AND LITHOSPHERE

Over 40 miles (64 km) deep! That's how thick Earth's crust is in some locations. As the solid covering of a rocky planet, the crust is composed of various rocks and minerals.

### FUN FACT

Beneath the lithosphere, the **asthenosphere** is the area of the upper mantle where rock "flows" very slowly due to high heat and pressure. The asthenosphere's convection currents create movement in the plates of the lithosphere above.

Earth's **crust** is actually the planet's thinnest layer when compared to the mantle and core beneath it. But the crust is home to all living things on Earth. Together with the **upper layer of the mantle**, Earth's crust forms the **lithosphere**, a section of the planet known for the massive movement of tectonic plates.

## Classifying Crust

Earth's crust fits into one of two categories—continental and oceanic. **Continental crust** is thicker and believed to be older than **oceanic crust**. Its average thickness is over 20 miles (32 km) deep. Continental crust contains granite-type rock with silicate and aluminum minerals. Oceanic crust, under the world's oceans, is very dense but only reaches approximately 6 miles (10 km) in depth. Created at mid-ocean ridges where magma rises and cools, oceanic crust is made of basalt rock and contains many silicate and magnesium minerals.

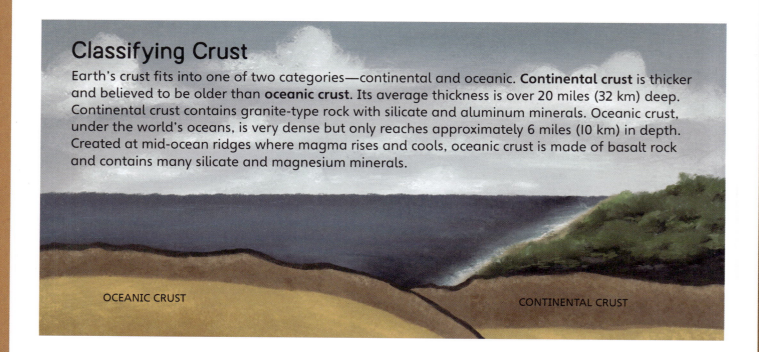

NATURE SCHOOL: PLANET EARTH

# The Continents

What is considered a **continent**? Expansive and continuous landmasses, often culturally distinct from one another, are considered continents. Seven continents are recognized on Earth: Asia, Africa, North America, South America, Antarctica, Europe, and Australia, often referred to as Oceania. While coastlines may appear to act as a border for continents, the continental shelf that extends out from the continent under the ocean water is actually the boundary.

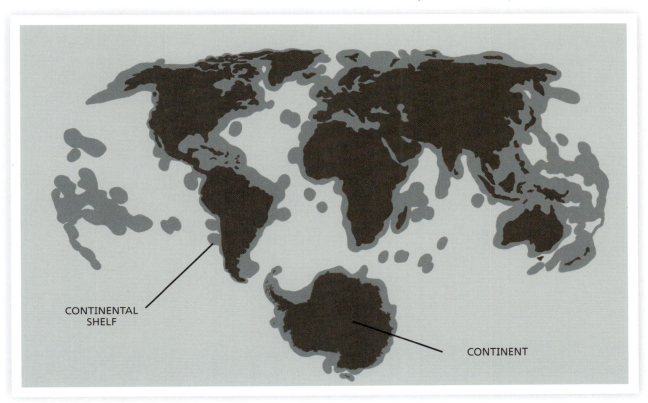

## FUN FACT

The Rock Cycle: **Sedimentary rocks** form when layers of eroded sediment are compacted together over time. **Igneous rocks** are created when molten magma cools and hardens. **Metamorphic rocks** are rocks that have changed form because of intense heat and pressure.

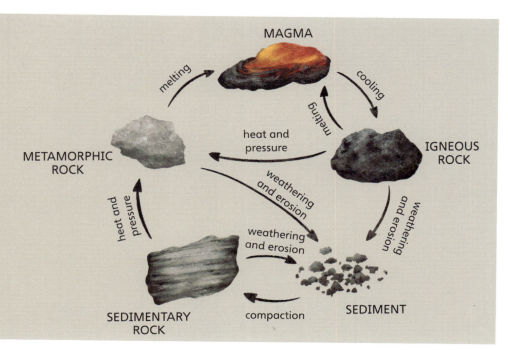

EARTH'S COMPOSITION

# EARTH'S PEDOSPHERE

The prominent **pedosphere** covers the outermost layer of Earth's crust where soil is actively forming. This layer supplies nutrients and water for plants in addition to acting as a substrate in which they can grow. It provides homes for animals and microorganisms as well. And soil filters water and stores minerals. Weathering of rocks by wind, water, and other factors creates soil over time as the rocks break down.

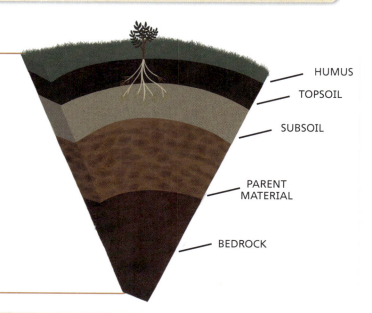

## Pedogenesis: Soil Formation

STEP 1: Soil formation begins with parent material, usually bedrock or sediments deposited by glaciers or streams.

STEP 2: The parent material is broken down by wind, rainwater, or freezing and thawing of water in the rocks. Plants such as mosses and lichens grow on the rocks.

STEP 3: Chemicals from decaying plants break down the rock. Organic matter begins to build up in the new soil from animals and plants.

STEP 4: A healthy soil profile forms with water, microorganisms, organic matter, and minerals from the rock to support plant and animal life.

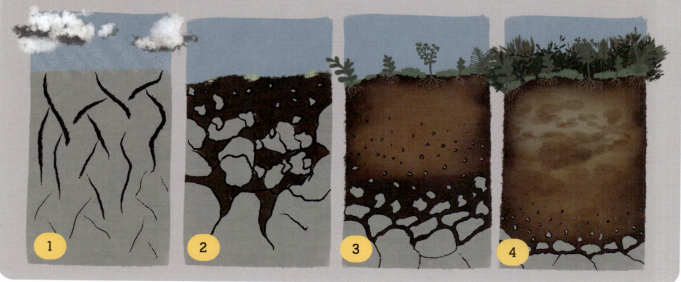

## A Selection of Soil

CHALKY soils are often shallow and contain calcium carbonate from sediment. They are alkaline in nature and drain quickly.

CLAY soils are slow to drain and hold water. Made of tiny particles, clay soil can be dense and easily compacted.

LOAM is a mixture of sand, silt, and clay. It can be nutrient rich and hold moisture, but it still drains well.

PEAT is an acidic soil that holds moisture and contains lots of organic matter.

SAND has large particles and drains quickly. Sandy soil does not hold its structure and is easily eroded.

SILT is fertile soil with medium-size particles. It holds moisture well, but its fine texture can be eroded by water.

### FUN FACT

Peat has been known to preserve ancient plant and animal fossils because of its high acidity and lack of oxygen needed for decomposition.

## Soil Microorganisms

One teaspoon of soil may contain up to 10,000 species of **microorganisms** such as bacteria, fungi, and protozoa. These microbes cycle nutrients through the soil and help plants to grow.

EARTH'S COMPOSITION

# PLATE TECTONICS: EARTH'S MOVING PARTS

While Earth's surface may seem static, it is actually moving! This slow motion is caused by heat from molten rock flowing under Earth's surface in a layer called the mantle. Not only is Earth moving beneath us, it's also divided into several large sections called plates. These aren't like dinner plates that you use for meals but rather large pieces of Earth's lithosphere that fit together like a prodigious puzzle. **Plate tectonics** is the theory describing this movement. It's an important concept because it explains how landforms such as mountains and trenches form and helps scientists understand more about potential natural disasters from earthquakes and volcanoes.

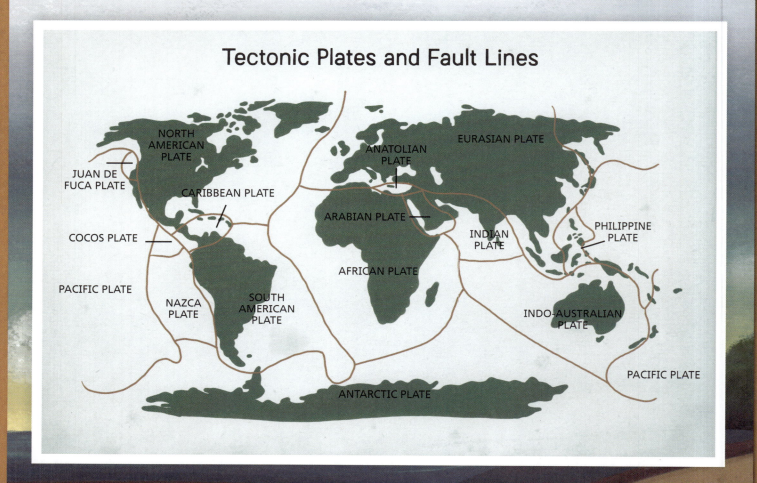

NATURE SCHOOL: PLANET EARTH

# Plate Boundaries

When plates in the lithosphere meet, different types of boundaries form depending on the action of the plates. Keep in mind that plates are so large that more than one type of boundary may form along their edges.

DIVERGENT BOUNDARIES form when plates move away from each other. Magma from under the surface may emerge as the plates separate, forming mid-ocean ridges in the oceans and rift valleys on land.

DIVERGENT

CONVERGENT BOUNDARIES form when plates meet or converge. This can cause Earth's crust to crinkle and move upward, forming steep mountain ranges. Subduction zones may also occur when plates converge, with one plate slipping under the other to form trenches.

CONVERGENT

TRANSFORM BOUNDARIES form when plates slide by each other instead of moving away or meeting. This can cause crust to wear away or break, and earthquakes are common along these edges.

TRANSFORM

CONTINENTAL CRUST

LITHOSPHERE
(UPPER MANTLE AND CRUST)

UPPER MANTLE

ASTHENOSPHERE

EARTH'S COMPOSITION
47

# HOW MOUNTAINS ARE MADE

Earth's surface is a work in progress. **Geological processes** such as earthquakes, erosion, sedimentation, soil formation, volcanic eruptions, and tectonic-plate movements contribute to the creation of new features on an ever-changing planet. Many of Earth's layers, from the upper mantle to the atmosphere, are involved in transforming the land. Some processes take place quickly, while others take many years.

## Earthquakes

When Earth's crust shakes, it's due to a quake! The movement of the tectonic plates that make up Earth's surface can cause an earthquake. While the plates move constantly at a very slow pace, they can get stuck. When they finally push past each other in a sudden movement, energy is released in seismic waves, resulting in an **earthquake**. The earthquake's magnitude is based on how long it lasts and how powerful the waves are. Earthquakes can cause changes in the planet's surface, such as cracks in the ground and ridge formation. They can also lead to mountains growing in height and rivers changing course.

### FUN FACT

Extending nearly 25,000 miles (40,000 km) in the Pacific Ocean, the **Ring of Fire** is home to approximately 450 volcanoes. With lots of movement between the Pacific Plate and those surrounding it in this region, earthquakes happen regularly.

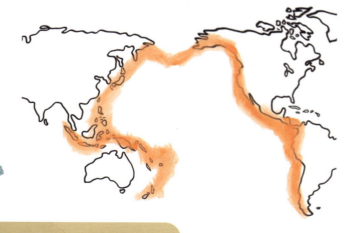

NATURE SCHOOL: PLANET EARTH
48

# Volcanoes

While **volcanoes** can be destructive, they can also add nutrients to the land around them and form mountains and islands as eruptions build up debris and ash. A volcano forms where molten rock underground called magma is under pressure and makes its way to Earth's surface through a vent in the crust. Magma may explode violently from the volcano, or it may flow from an effusive volcano.

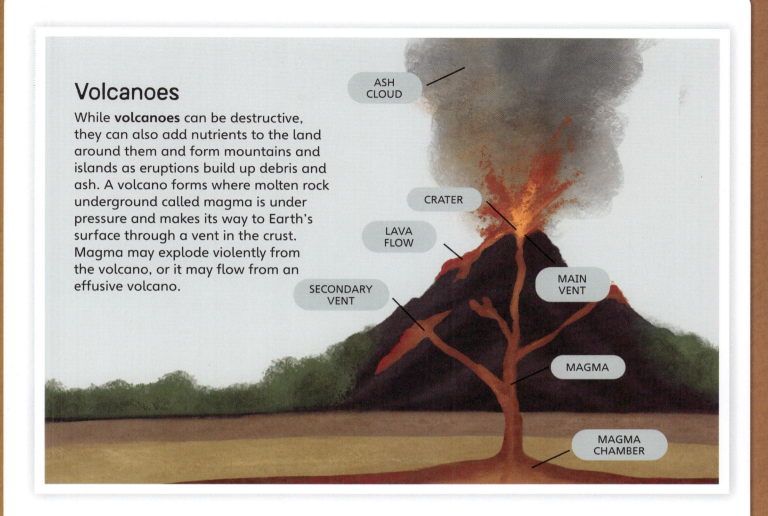

## Types of Volcanoes

CINDER CONE VOLCANOES are a common type of volcano with steep sides and a crater at the top and are formed when exploding magma falls down and builds up around a single vent.

SHIELD VOLCANOES are large and broad. Their gently sloping sides form when lava flows from the vent.

STRATOVOLCANOES, also known as composite volcanoes, are tall with steep sides and form when lava, ash, and cinders build up around it. Lava may flow from fissures along the sides of the main vent.

LAVA DOME VOLCANOES form when thick lava flows very slowly, forming a dome over the top.

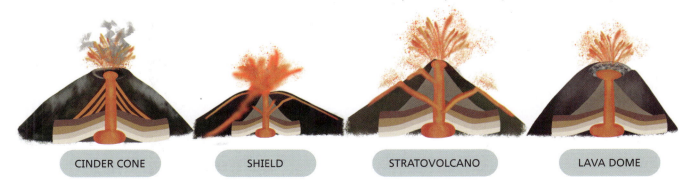

EARTH'S COMPOSITION

# EARTH'S GEOLOGICAL CHARACTERISTICS

Earth has distinctive characteristics that shape its surface. These features form over time, creating beautiful and distinctive landscapes. Many processes help form Earth's surface.

1. **WEATHERING** breaks down rocks, and sediment is carried away and deposited in new areas. Precipitation adds water to the landscape and creates more chances for both physical and chemical weathering to occur.
2. **GLACIAL MOVEMENT** creates landforms as giant sections of ice cut into mountains, forge valleys and fjords, create lakes and kettles, and deposit rock and sediment far from its origin.
3. **FLUVIAL PROCESSES** move sediments via river flow. These sediments may be deposited as sandbars or alongside rivers in natural levees, and they may create oxbow lakes as rivers meander.
4. **IGNEOUS PROCESSES** form volcanoes, mountains, domes, and plateaus on Earth's surface as lava cools and creates these new landforms.
5. **TECTONIC PROCESSES** move the plates that make up Earth's crust. As they move away from each other, collide, or slide past each other, they create landforms such as mountains, trenches, islands, and volcanoes.
6. **HILLSLOPES**, whether bare rock or covered in vegetation, allow sediment to be carried away downhill, sometimes helped along by water.
7. **MARINE PROCESSES** affect the coast, wearing away rock to create cliffs, headlands, and other landforms. They also deposit rocks and sand to form beaches.

NATURE SCHOOL: PLANET EARTH

## Topography

The shape of Earth's surface and its landforms is known as **topography**. The elevation and contour of an area change with mountains and valleys, plains and canyons. Topography influences the ecosystems that will form in a region, which in turn impacts the plants and animals that can live there.

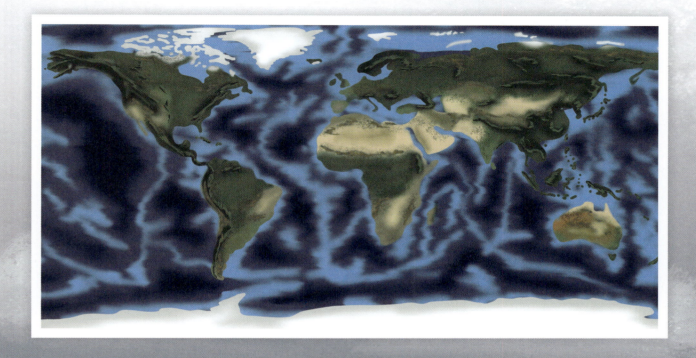

EARTH'S COMPOSITION
51

# EARTH'S NATURAL WONDERS

Different types of **landforms** make up Earth's terrain, from deep canyons to flat plains to mountain peaks and everything in between. Landforms may be visible on Earth's surface, but they also exist deep within the ocean. Formed by geological processes such as tectonic-plate movement, weathering, and erosion, Earth's spectacular features make for a dynamic landscape.

## MOUNTAINS

**MOUNTAINS** often form when plates collide or when magma pushes up to Earth's surface and cools. With steep sides rising from the ocean floor or towering over the surrounding land, mountains are at least 1,000 feet (305 m) tall and have a peak.

## CANYONS

**CANYONS** are cut through the land by rivers and glaciers as they weather rock and carry it away. Both deep and narrow, canyon walls may rise thousands of feet.

NATURE SCHOOL: PLANET EARTH

## DESERTS

**DESERTS** are arid ecosystems with little water for flora and fauna. Deserts often form when air circulating over them has already lost its moisture while traveling across mountains or tropical areas.

## BEACHES

**BEACHES** may be covered in rocks, sand, or mud, and they are created by deposits of sediment brought in by the tide. The same waves that create the beach can also remove sediment as the beach changes daily.

## CAVES

**CAVES** are natural openings on Earth, usually formed when soluble rock such as limestone is worn away over time by a solution of carbon dioxide and water flowing through the ground.

EARTH'S COMPOSITION

## ISLANDS

**ISLANDS** are bodies of land completely surrounded by water. Some islands form when continents separate or from variations in sea level. Others are created by glacial deposits or by volcano tops emerging above the water's surface.

## PLAINS

PLAINS are expanses of flat land. Formed by flowing water, glacial movements, or lava flows from volcanic eruptions, plains cover approximately one-third of Earth's surface.

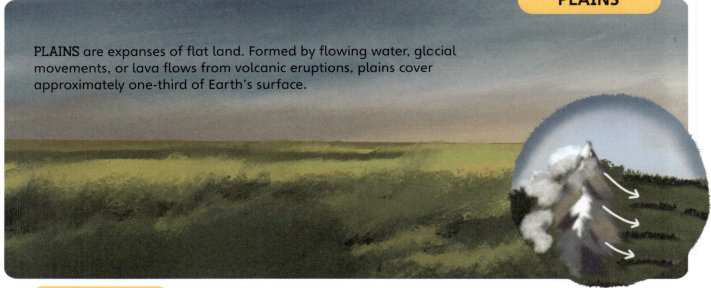

## PLATEAUS

PLATEAUS are elevated areas of level ground formed when tectonic plates collide and raise up Earth's crust. Lava flows can also build up plateaus over time.

## VALLEYS

**VALLEYS** can be wide and shallow or narrow and steep-walled depending on whether they form in mountains or across plains. Formed by rivers or glaciers that weather the land, valleys are lowland areas.

## CLIFFS

**CLIFFS** form along the coast or along mountains. Precipitation, wind, and ocean waves can weather rocks and cause erosion that leaves a sheer, nearly vertical rock feature.

## HILLS

**HILLS** rise above the surrounding land and usually have a summit, though they are smaller than mountains. They can be formed by plate tectonics or by erosion and sediment deposits.

# ACTIVITIES

Throughout chapter two, you explored Earth's composition. From the layers deep within Earth to natural landforms and how they develop, you've studied the geological processes that give Earth its unique characteristics. Now, you have the chance to review what you've learned through these hands-on activities and research opportunities.

## Nature Journal

Choose a specific landform you would like to study further, preferably one you can visit in the region where you live. This could be a mountain or range, volcano, ridge, valley, or any other formation created through geological processes. Research to discover information about it, such as its location, when and how it formed, and whether it has changed over time. In your nature journal, record this information along with an illustration or photograph of the landform.

## Earth's Layers

Make a miniature model of Earth! Using different colors of playdough or clay, you can create a tiny version of Earth's layers, which you learned about in this chapter. You'll need to construct the following layers: inner core, outer core, mantle, and crust. We recommend using red for the inner core, yellow for the outer core, orange for the mantle, and blue with green "land" areas for the outermost crust layer. Start by making a small sphere of red for the inner core, approximately 1 inch (2.5 cm) across. For the following steps, make a ball with each color of playdough, and then roll it out into a flat circle to wrap around the previous spheres. Cover the inner core with a layer of yellow for the outer core. Then, cover the yellow layer with orange for the mantle. Finally, layer the blue followed by green continents. Your model will look like a mini globe. Cut through your sphere with a sharp knife, taking care not to flatten the model while cutting. All the layers should be revealed upon slicing it open. See if you can name each one!

NATURE SCHOOL: PLANET EARTH

## Rock and Roll

Next time you're on a nature walk, be sure to collect some smooth rocks to use for this rock-painting activity. Gather a variety of shapes and sizes. Then, use acrylic paints or paint markers to decorate your rocks. You can make your rocks look like your favorite animals or people, add colors and patterns, or write words or names on them. Or you can always make up your own creative designs.

## It's Gonna Blow!

You've learned how volcanoes form through plate tectonics, and now you can construct your very own volcano and make it erupt. You'll need an empty plastic water or soda bottle, one packet of quick-rise yeast, half a cup of hydrogen peroxide, a funnel, and a sandbox, dirt pile, or snow. Gather your supplies, and take them all outdoors. Carefully pour the yeast into your plastic bottle. Then, without spilling the yeast, form a volcano of sand, mud, or snow around your bottle. Be sure to keep the bottle opening visible so you can add your hydrogen peroxide in the next step. Once your volcano is formed, pour the hydrogen peroxide into the bottle, and wait for the eruption! Alternatively, you could use vinegar and baking soda for your "lava." You could also add red or orange food coloring to make it look more like lava.

# ACTIVITIES

## Orange-Peel Plate Tectonics

Visualizing plate tectonics—how Earth's plates fit together and move—can be challenging. This activity will help you see the things you read about Earth's lithosphere in this chapter. You'll just need an orange. Using your fingers, carefully remove the peel from the orange in a handful of pieces—you can even try to make 7 sections to represent the major plates on Earth. After you peel the orange, try to fit the "plates" back around it. The round orange represents Earth while the pieces of peel represent the tectonic plates of the lithosphere. You learned that tectonic plates are always moving over the asthenosphere, and now you can test it out. Can you see the exposed mantle when the orange peel plates diverge? Do the plates buckle, or is a trench created when the plates collide?

## Centrifugal Force

A spinning Earth is responsible for night and day. Earth makes one rotation every 24 hours. You learned that Earth is not a perfect sphere, and the middle of the planet bulges outward as it rotates. This is due to centrifugal force, which means an object moving in a circle is likely to travel away from the circle's center. You can demonstrate this by using a small, soft toy and a string. Simply cut a string about 3 feet (1 m) long, and tie it securely around the toy. Go outside or to an open space, and hold on to the loose end of the string. Because of gravity, the toy will dangle toward the ground. Swing the string around in a circle, and observe what happens to the toy. It flies up and outward away from you due to centrifugal force. So, why don't we fly off of Earth as it rotates in a circle? Thanks to gravity, we remain on Earth's surface.

## Fossil Hunting

As Earth changes through different geological processes, fossils can be buried under layers of sediment, sand, or peat. You can go fossil hunting to find fossils that have been buried for many years. You'll need permission to collect fossils, or you can just observe them without collecting. Take along a magnifying glass, flashlight, and notebook to record when and where you found the fossils. If you're planning to collect, a small hammer and chisel, safety glasses, and a container in which to store the fossils are necessary. The best places for fossil hunting usually have exposed layers of sedimentary rock, like rocky outcrops. Peat bogs may have fossils to find as well. Marine and cave habitats can also be great places to look!

## Layers of Sediment

Chapter two referred to weathering of rocks and erosion of sediment and how these processes change the shape of Earth's surface when sediment is deposited in new locations. Now you can make your own sediment jar! You'll need a plastic jar with a lid, soil, sand, gravel, and water. Add a small scoop of the soil, sand, and gravel to your jar, then fill it almost to the top with water. Secure the lid to the jar, then shake it up and watch the sediment fall. Record your observations of the different sediment layers.

## Did You Know?

Mt. Everest boasts the world's highest peak, which sits just over 29,000 feet (9 km) above sea level. When measured from sea level, Ecuador's Mt. Chimborazo is just over 20,500 feet (6 km). However, because Mt. Chimborazo is near the equator and centrifugal force causes Earth to bulge around the middle, Mt. Chimborazo is actually farther from Earth's center than Mt. Everest by almost 7,000 feet (2 km).

EARTH'S COMPOSITION

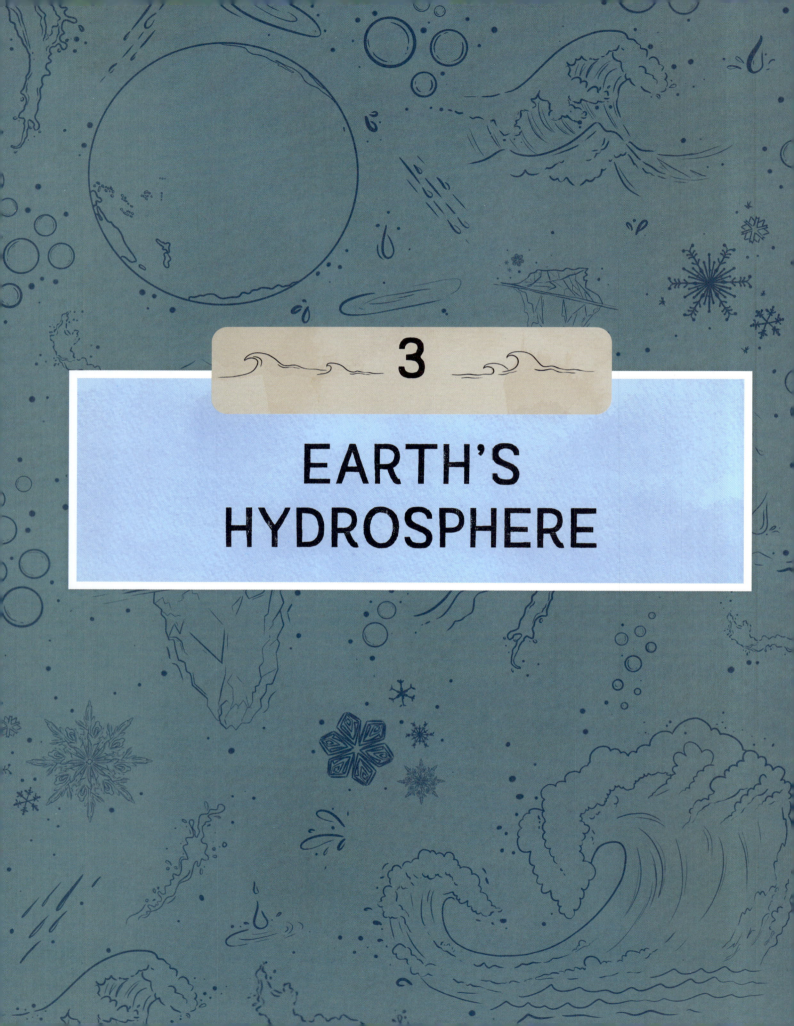

# 3

# EARTH'S HYDROSPHERE

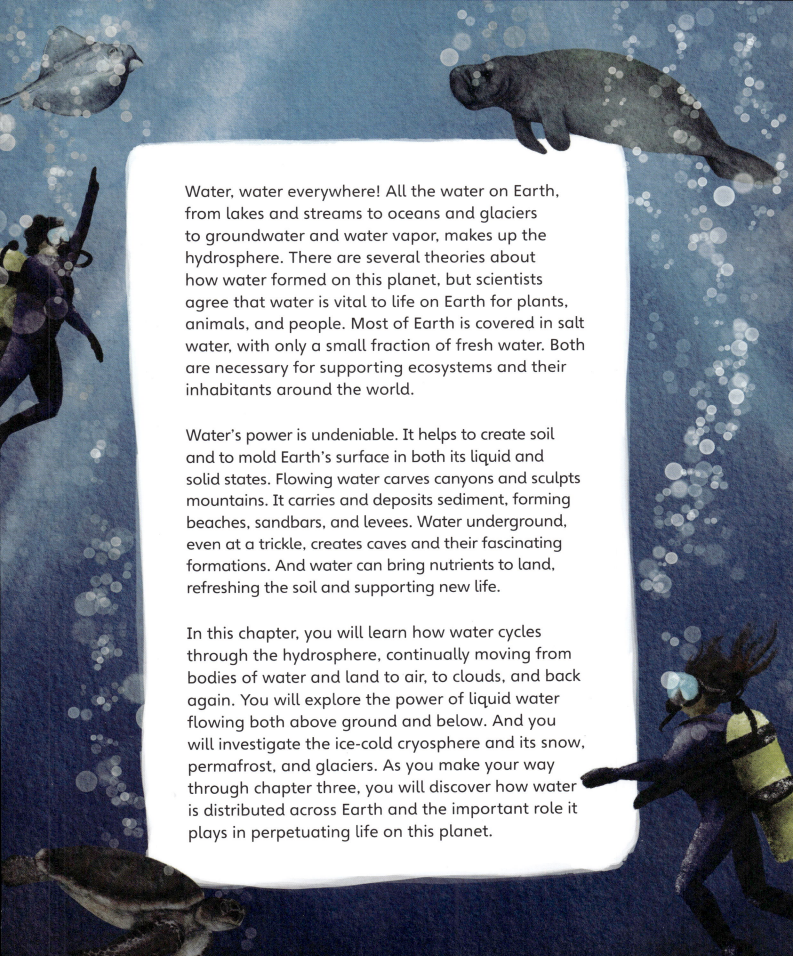

Water, water everywhere! All the water on Earth, from lakes and streams to oceans and glaciers to groundwater and water vapor, makes up the hydrosphere. There are several theories about how water formed on this planet, but scientists agree that water is vital to life on Earth for plants, animals, and people. Most of Earth is covered in salt water, with only a small fraction of fresh water. Both are necessary for supporting ecosystems and their inhabitants around the world.

Water's power is undeniable. It helps to create soil and to mold Earth's surface in both its liquid and solid states. Flowing water carves canyons and sculpts mountains. It carries and deposits sediment, forming beaches, sandbars, and levees. Water underground, even at a trickle, creates caves and their fascinating formations. And water can bring nutrients to land, refreshing the soil and supporting new life.

In this chapter, you will learn how water cycles through the hydrosphere, continually moving from bodies of water and land to air, to clouds, and back again. You will explore the power of liquid water flowing both above ground and below. And you will investigate the ice-cold cryosphere and its snow, permafrost, and glaciers. As you make your way through chapter three, you will discover how water is distributed across Earth and the important role it plays in perpetuating life on this planet.

# THE BLUE PLANET

With over two-thirds of the planet covered in water, it's not surprising that Earth's nickname is "the blue planet." Earth's cerulean appearance from space is largely due to its salty seas. While the name "Earth" comes from a word that means "ground," it is most definitely an ocean planet. The large amount of liquid surface water covering Earth is unique among planets studied by scientists. While other bodies in the solar system may have ice or subsurface water, Earth is just far enough from the Sun that much of its surface water remains liquid.

### FUN FACT

Earth is likely not the only place in our solar system with water. Mars, Pluto, planetary moons, comets, and asteroids are believed to have different forms of water, such as ice, water vapor, and possibly subsurface liquid water.

EARTH CENTERED ON THE PACIFIC OCEAN SIDE

## The Dynamic Hydrosphere

Earth's **hydrosphere** holds all of its water on land, in the air, and underground. Water in the hydrosphere may be in different states, whether gas, liquid, or solid. Water regularly cycles through Earth and its atmosphere, evaporating from the ground, forming clouds, and falling back down as precipitation.

### FUN FACT

One theory of the formation of water on Earth hypothesizes that asteroids pelting Earth early in its existence brought with them hydrogen and oxygen, the components needed to form water.

NATURE SCHOOL: PLANET EARTH
62

## Where's the Water?

Where is most of Earth's water found? If you guessed the oceans, you are spot on! Earth's marine habitats make up 97 percent of the planet's water. Fresh water is necessary for life, but it's only a tiny fraction of all the water on this planet. A small amount of fresh water is found in lakes and rivers. Most fresh water is underground or in frozen areas like glaciers and ice caps, known as the cryosphere.

- OCEANS 96.5%
- GLACIERS 1.7%
- GROUNDWATER 1.7%
- LAKES 0.013%
- RIVERS 0.002%
- SOIL 0.001%
- ATMOSPHERE 0.001%
- BIOLOGICAL 0.001% (IN LIVING THINGS)

## Water Is Life

Earth's surface, where life is found, is mostly covered in water. Water is needed by all living things, from the smallest microbe to the largest plants and animals. Humans need water to carry nutrients through their body, maintain their cell structure, eliminate waste, protect joints and organs, and keep their body temperature constant. Plants use water to maintain their shape, photosynthesize, and take in nutrients from the soil. With water's ability to act as a solvent, it plays an important role in many chemical reactions in living organisms. Plus, water's transparency allows light to pass through it. It also conducts heat, and its molecules have a high surface tension.

EARTH'S HYDROSPHERE

# THE WATER CYCLE

Water constantly moves through Earth and the atmosphere in a cycle. On this planet, water is stored as liquid, solid, or gas on land, in the ground, and in the atmosphere. While water is vital to all living things, it moves through ecosystems differently depending on factors such as their climate, terrain, flora, and fauna. All habitable regions on Earth must have at least some water. Rainforests, along with freshwater and saltwater ecosystems, have the most moisture while deserts, tundra, and savannas can be quite dry.

## Water on the Move

The **water cycle** describes the path that water takes as it moves around the planet. You can start at any point in the water cycle to follow the path that water takes. For example, liquid water in a lake heats up from the Sun and **evaporates** as water vapor into the air. As the water vapor rises and cools, it **condenses** to form a cloud in the sky. When the cloud becomes saturated, **precipitation** such as rain or snow falls back to Earth. This water may sink into the ground or run off into a river, lake, or ocean, where the cycle begins again. The water cycle impacts weather systems around the globe.

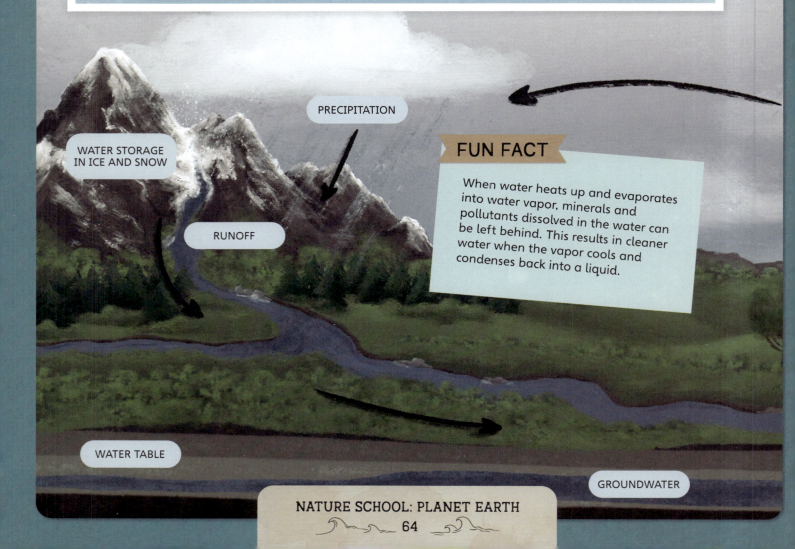

### FUN FACT

When water heats up and evaporates into water vapor, minerals and pollutants dissolved in the water can be left behind. This results in cleaner water when the vapor cools and condenses back into a liquid.

NATURE SCHOOL: PLANET EARTH

# Water Storage

Water is stored in natural **reservoirs** on Earth. These may be cold or warm, and the water may be stored as ice, liquid water, or water vapor. The water cycle describes water's movement between these storage areas.

> **FUN FACT**
>
> A drop of water may spend thousands of years in the deep ocean before evaporating into the atmosphere, while a drop of water in a warm, shallow area may evaporate relatively quickly.

Earth's largest reservoir is its **oceans**, which stores approximately 97 percent of all water on the planet.

As a liquid, fresh water is stored in **lakes**, **rivers**, **wetlands**, and **underground** in aquifers or in soil.

Fresh water is also stored frozen in **glaciers** and large **ice sheets**, and **snowpack** at high elevations also acts as a fresh water reservoir.

**Water vapor** is found in the atmosphere above both land and sea.

CLOUDS AND VAPOR

TRANSPIRATION

CONDENSATION

EVAPORATION

WATER STORAGE IN OCEAN

**EARTH'S HYDROSPHERE**

# PROPERTIES OF WATER

Water is one of the most important things on planet Earth! It's found all over the world, from huge oceans full of salt water to tiny puddles on the sidewalk. Water naturally exists as a solid in ice and snow, as a liquid in bodies of water, and as a gas in water vapor. Its density, or the mass that a specific volume of water weighs, is around 1 gram per milliliter. But water's density varies with temperature. Usually solids are denser than liquids, but water is unique in that its frozen state is less dense than liquid water.

## The Magnificent Molecule

Water is the most prevalent molecule on Earth. Each water molecule has two atoms of **hydrogen** and one atom of **oxygen** bonded together. In this bond, they share electrons, but not equally. The oxygen atom attracts the electrons more strongly, so that side of the molecule is slightly negative, like the charge on electrons. This means the hydrogen side of the molecule is more positive. With negative and positive sides, water molecules are considered polar. The positive side of a water molecule is attracted to the negative side of another water molecule, and vice versa. And they are also attracted to other substances, so water can easily dissolve many other substances, including the minerals and nutrients valuable to living organisms.

### FUN FACT

Water has a high heat capacity, meaning it takes a lot of energy to raise its temperature. Earth's climate is influenced by water's high heat capacity because water does not heat up or cool off as quickly as land does, keeping many coastal regions mild and less prone to extreme temperatures between seasons when compared to inland regions.

NATURE SCHOOL: PLANET EARTH

## States of Water

Water exists in liquid, solid, and gas forms in nature. From lakes to glaciers to water vapor in the air, each state of water has different characteristics.

While **liquid** water flows and is fluid with molecules moving around, solid water behaves much differently.

Ice forms a uniform crystalline structure with its molecules spread apart in an orderly fashion. This results in **solid** ice being less dense, which means ice can float in liquid water.

Water can also be a **gas**, like water vapor, which forms as water evaporates from the surface of bodies of water and transpires from plant leaves. Less dense than both liquid and solid water, water vapor molecules are spread farther apart from each other.

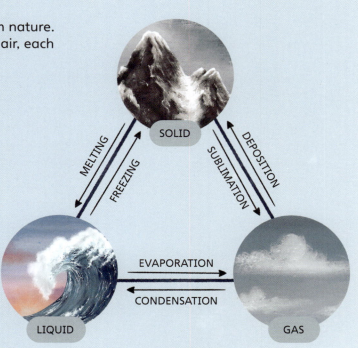

## Stick Together

With two atoms of hydrogen and one atom of oxygen in each water molecule, water's chemical symbol is $H_2O$. Water's polar structure and its tendency to bond with other water molecules makes it "sticky," or cohesive. Water molecules' **cohesion**, or the ability to stick to each other, is what allows water droplets to form. Cohesion also creates surface tension as demonstrated in nature by the ability of water striders to walk across the surface of a stream without sinking in. The ability for water molecules to stick to other substances is called **adhesion**, which is evident in water climbing up the walls of plant vessels.

### FUN FACT

Pure water, in which nothing is dissolved, will not conduct electricity. However, most water contains free ions (charged atoms) from molecules that have been dissolved by the water, allowing electricity to flow.

EARTH'S HYDROSPHERE

# SALT WATER: EARTH'S OCEANS

One global ocean surrounds planet Earth and covers over 70 percent of its surface. Traditionally, the ocean is divided into 5 geographical regions, with the Pacific being the largest, followed by the Atlantic, Indian, Southern, and Arctic. The salty ocean makes up approximately 97 percent of all the water on Earth. And because the ocean is so vast, its currents influence the climate around the globe, bringing warm water from the equator to the poles and cold water back toward the equator.

## The World's Oceans

The average depth of the ocean is around 12,000 feet (4 km), but the deepest recesses plunge to over 35,000 feet (11 km) in the Mariana Trench. Despite the vastness of the ocean and all the life it contains, scientists have mapped only a fraction of the seafloor and explored even less. One of the most commonly known characteristics of the ocean is its salinity. Most salts make their way to the ocean from rivers flowing over rocks on land, breaking them down and carrying the minerals with them as they travel to the ocean. On average, the salinity of ocean water is around 35 parts per 1,000. Some areas may have decreased salinity, such as the surface water of the tropics near the equator, where rain falls in abundance. Regions with lots of evaporation and little fresh water being added will have higher salinity.

### FUN FACT

The words **"ocean"** and **"sea"** are often used as if they were the same thing; however, seas are smaller sections of the ocean near land and are often partially enclosed.

NATURE SCHOOL: PLANET EARTH

# Ocean in Motion

**Currents** move water through the ocean around planet Earth. Similar to the flow of rivers, currents follow paths around the world. Currents vary in depth from surface to deep water, and some are even large enough to be named. The Kuroshio Current in the Pacific near Japan and the Gulf Stream in the Atlantic near the United States are two examples of important currents carrying warm water northward. Currents can be caused by wind near the surface of the water and by temperature and salinity differences in the ocean. The **Coriolis effect**, caused by the rotation of Earth, influences ocean currents to bend away from the equator to the right in the Northern Hemisphere and to the left in the Southern Hemisphere.

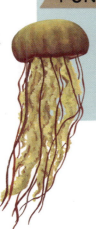

### FUN FACT

The **biodiversity**, or variety of life, in the ocean is unknown because of the vastness of the ocean and the fact that so much of it remains unexplored. Scientists have identified over 240,000 different species of ocean plants and animals. Biodiversity is important for ocean ecosystems to be successful even if environmental factors change.

EARTH'S HYDROSPHERE

69

# SEABED: THE LANDSCAPE OF THE OCEAN

Land at the bottom of the ocean—near the surface in shallow water or far below in the deepest ocean zone—is called the seabed, seafloor, or ocean floor. While difficult to explore in many places because of the water pressure, darkness, and cold temperatures, the ocean floor has similar features and landforms as the continents. Seagrasses may grow on the ocean floor in shallow areas where sunlight allows them to photosynthesize.

## Where Land Meets Ocean

The **continental margin** spans the edges of continents out into the deep water of the ocean. Usually, **continental shelves** are gently sloping areas of the continental margin from the shore to the shelf break, where the **continental slope** merges with the deep ocean. The **continental rise** forms at the edge of the continental slope, where sediment from the continent is carried out to sea and deposited.

Much like the continental crust, oceanic crust features a variety of landforms: massive mountain ridges, treacherous deep-sea **trenches**, cavernous caves, and amazing abyssal plains. New crust emerges at the **mid-ocean ridges**. Deep trenches are created where plates in the crust get pushed beneath other plates. Underwater **volcanoes** form where magma comes up from spaces between plates, hardening and piling up over time. **Abyssal plains** often form past the continental rise, as sediment such as sand and silt along with decaying organic matter cover the crust.

SHORE
CONTINENTAL SHELF
CONTINENTAL MARGIN
CONTINENTAL SLOPE
CONTINENTAL RISE
TRENCH
ABYSSAL PLAIN
OCEANIC CRUST

NATURE SCHOOL: PLANET EARTH

## The Deep

Below the ocean surface at 600 feet (183 m), where light begins to fade, lies the deep ocean. Beyond 3,000 feet (1 km), darkness dominates, water is cold, and pressure is intense. But . . . there is life! The **epipelagic zone** teems with phytoplankton, marine mammals, and fish. The next zone is the **mesopelagic zone**, which does not allow for photosynthesis with its lack of sunlight and where fish along with tiny krill and squid are at home. Even deeper is the **bathypelagic zone**, a cold, dark, and pressure-filled place. Creatures here feed on marine snow and a mixture of waste and decaying organic matter drifting down from the zones above. Fish and octopuses adapted to great pressure make their home in the **abyssopelagic zone**, found on the floor of the abyssal plain. Finally, the **hadalpelagic zone** goes all the way to the bottom of deep-ocean trenches.

### FUN FACT

Submarine vehicles carrying humans have ventured all the way to the ocean's deepest point, the Challenger Deep in the Mariana Trench, over 35,800 feet (11 km) below the water's surface.

MID-OCEAN RIDGE

MOUNTAIN RIDGE

VOLCANO

EARTH'S HYDROSPHERE

# EARTH'S FRESH WATER

Planet Earth may be the "blue planet," but most of the world's water is salt water. Fresh water makes up just 3 percent of all the water on Earth! And much of the world's fresh water sits in ice sheets and glaciers or underground. Fresh water is also found in rivers and streams, wetlands, lakes and ponds, water vapor, and clouds.

## What Is a Lake?

**Lakes** are bodies of water surrounded by land, often formed in low-lying areas when runoff from the surrounding watershed fills them up or when a spring empties into them. Most lakes are freshwater, but some saltwater lakes exist. Lakes vary greatly in size and productivity level, which refers to the plant and animal life they support. Shallow, mucky, sometimes green lakes with lots of plants growing and animals living in them are classified as **eutrophic**. Usually clear, **oligotrophic** lakes have less productivity due to a lack of nutrients in the water. **Mesotrophic** lakes are in between the other two in their productivity levels, with some plant life to support more creatures.

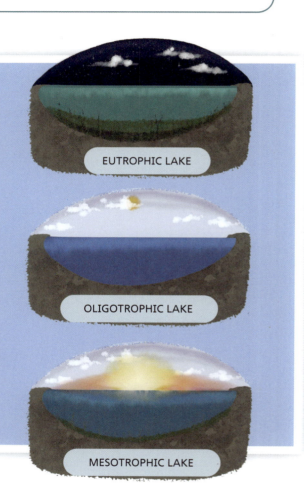

EUTROPHIC LAKE

OLIGOTROPHIC LAKE

MESOTROPHIC LAKE

### FUN FACT

Ponds are generally smaller and shallower than lakes and may have plants growing through the entire water body. Lakes are usually too deep for plants in some areas, and they may stratify into layers during the warm season.

NATURE SCHOOL: PLANET EARTH

# Rivers

**Rivers**, along with smaller streams and creeks, fit into the category of lotic, or flowing water, ecosystems. Besides acting as a habitat for many plant and animal species, rivers carry water to the **ocean**, along with sediment from weathering. Rivers begin at a source such as melting snow or **glaciers**, **lakes**, or springs, and flow downhill. In its early stages, a river cuts a V-shaped **valley** and flows quickly down a steep slope. While it may begin as a small stream, rainwater and other **tributary** streams will add to it, creating a river system. As a river matures and more water is added to it, the river widens, and its flow slows. In old age, a river's valley is wider, with **floodplains** extending on either side. The **mouth** forms the river's end, where it meets a larger body of water. There, the river may release the silty sediments it carries, forming a **delta**.

## FUN FACT

Where freshwater rivers meet the salty ocean and the two waters mix, brackish water forms. Brackish water is saltier than fresh water, but it's not as salty as the ocean. Some animals, like bull sharks and oysters, are adapted to life in brackish water.

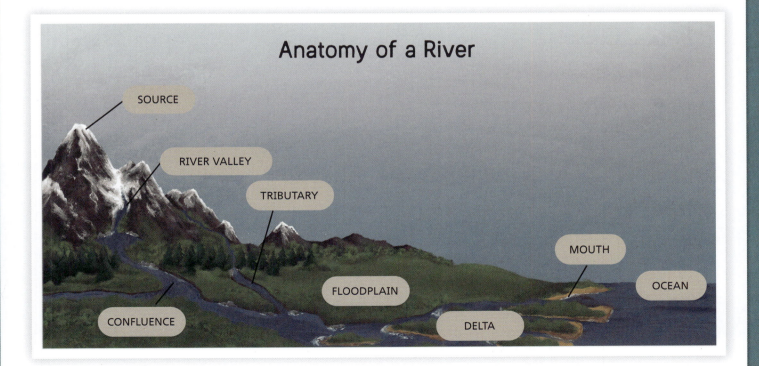

Anatomy of a River

EARTH'S HYDROSPHERE

# EARTH'S GROUNDWATER

Found in the spaces between rocks underground, **groundwater** is part of the water cycle. It infiltrates or soaks into the ground after precipitation like rain and snow falls from the clouds. There is much more water stored in the ground than in all the rivers and lakes on Earth's surface. Groundwater provides drinking water and irrigation in many areas of the world.

### FUN FACT

Groundwater that flows out onto the surface of Earth forms a spring. Spring water might trickle out slowly, or it might flow readily with thousands or even millions of gallons a day, forming pools.

## The Water Table

The **water table** is the border between **saturated** and **unsaturated** areas underground. Beneath the water table, groundwater fills the spaces created by pores and fractures in and between rocks. This is called the saturated or phreatic zone and is bordered underneath by **impermeable rock**. Above the water table, there may be some water, but there are air spaces as well. Sometimes a **perched water table** forms over a small area of impermeable rock above the saturation zone. The water table usually follows the topography of the land on the surface, flowing downhill.

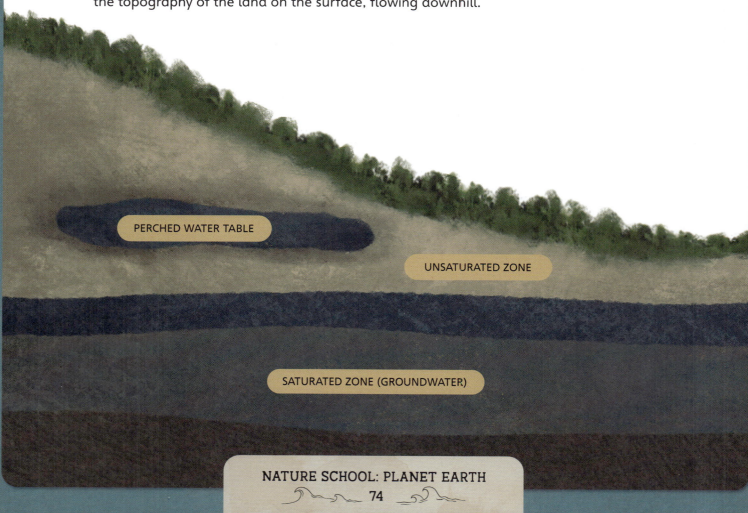

NATURE SCHOOL: PLANET EARTH

# Aquifers

**Aquifers** are areas of rock or sediment, such as gravel or limestone, underground that contain water. An aquifer is considered confined when it's trapped under clay or impermeable rock, while unconfined aquifers form under a permeable layer like soil. Springs are natural areas where water from aquifers comes out of Earth, but human-made wells can also be drilled into aquifers. Aquifers discharge when water leaves them, and they recharge when precipitation soaks into the ground.

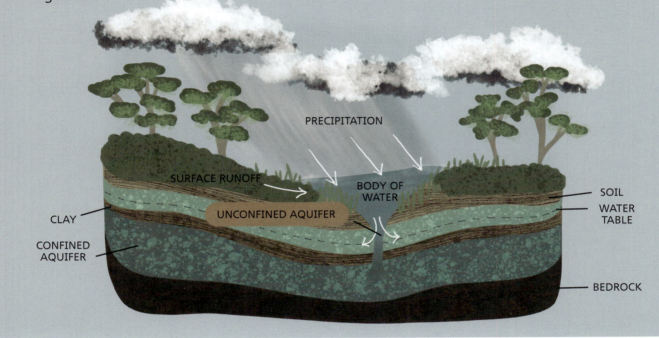

## FUN FACT

Fresh water can be found in the form of soil moisture, which allows plants to get the water they need to survive. Water infiltrates the soil from precipitation, like rain or melting snow. Soil with fine particles such as clay usually holds more water.

EARTH'S HYDROSPHERE

# EARTH'S CRYOSPHERE

From the Greek word "krios," meaning "cold," the cryosphere is made of the frozen water on planet Earth. Ice and snow are found in many areas of the world, including glaciers, ice sheets, ice in the ocean and other bodies of water, and permafrost in the tundra. The cryosphere impacts Earth's atmosphere by reflecting sunlight instead of absorbing it. When large areas of ice melt or build up, the air temperature and water currents around them may be affected.

## Ice Albedo

While land tends to absorb sunlight, ice on Earth's surface reflects light back into the atmosphere, keeping the planet cool. Albedo is the proportion, or fraction of light reflected by a surface. Ice and snow reflect a large proportion of the solar radiation they receive, so they have a high albedo.

### FUN FACT

Carbon is stored in permafrost from organic matter like plants and animals that didn't decompose completely before being frozen in the soil. Scientists estimate there is more carbon in the permafrost than in the atmosphere.

ICE CAP

GLACIER

SEA ICE

PERMAFROST

NATURE SCHOOL: PLANET EARTH

SNOW

SEA ICE

GLACIER

LAKE ICE

PERMAFROST

# Types of Ice

Ice forms in freshwater lakes and rivers, in the ocean, and also on land. Ice can be seasonal, melting each year, or it can remain year after year for thousands of years. **Snow** falls as precipitation usually at high elevations and in the mid and high latitudes. Snow cover reflects sunlight and provides insulation to the plants and animals underneath it, and melting snow can infiltrate the ground, giving moisture to the soil. **Sea ice** forms in the ocean in areas where the water is cold enough to freeze. It may melt again when temperatures warm up. Sections of sea ice are used by animals to hunt from and live under. **Glaciers** form in cold areas where at least some snowfall remains each year, so the snow builds up year after year on mountains and across continents. The pressure builds up on the buried snow, compressing it onto the glacier. Glacier movement creates landforms as the ice cuts through rock, carries sediments, and molds Earth's surface. **Ice sheets** are massive glaciers that blanket huge stretches of land. They store a large amount of Earth's fresh water. When these ice sheets extend out over the ocean, they are called **ice shelves**. Smaller ice sheets, less than 19,000 square miles (49,200 square km) in area, are known as **ice caps**. Large sections of ice may break off from glaciers and ice sheets, forming **icebergs**. **Permafrost** is frozen ground that remains frozen for at least 2 years. It can be made from rock, soil, or sand and is more common in cold climates where the average yearly temperature is below freezing, such as the high latitudes and high elevations.

## FUN FACT

The largest ice sheet in the world is the Antarctic ice sheet, extending over 5 million square miles (13 million square km) with an estimated volume of 6 billion cubic miles (25 billion cubic km).

ICEBERG

ICE SHELF

SNOW

EARTH'S HYDROSPHERE

# HOW WATER SHAPES EARTH

A powerful force, water has shaped Earth's landscape by **weathering** and **erosion**, carving rock and depositing sediment. From rivers running over the surface of the planet to waves crashing against the coastline, water transforms everything it touches. Abrasion weathers rock as water carries material that hits against it. Hydraulic action in waves pounds water and air into rock with crashing waves.

## Erosion

STEP 1: As waves pummel the land, the weakest areas of rock with cracks around the base are weathered first.

STEP 2: A small cave opening is created from repeated waves crashing into the rock.

STEP 3: The small opening becomes a natural arch, and sediment is carried away by the movement of the water.

STEP 4: Eventually, the arch grows large enough through weathering and erosion from both sides that it collapses, creating a rock stack.

NATURE SCHOOL: PLANET EARTH

## Flooding

Floods occur when heavy rains fall or when snow and ice melt quickly. Storm surges on the coast after a tropical storm cause flooding as well. When water flows onto land that is usually dry, it's considered a flood. Flooding can cause erosion of riverbanks and beaches and can carry sediment to new areas. Flooding can have positive impacts on land and can recharge aquifers to increase groundwater supplies. Flooding can also add nitrogen, phosphorus, and other nutrients to the soil to replenish ecosystems.

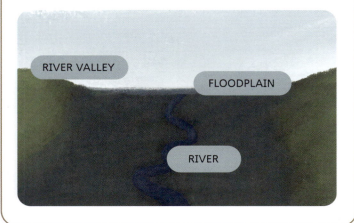

### FUN FACT

Dams build up reservoirs of river water behind them to use for homes, irrigation, and industry. They can also be used to generate electricity when the water is released and spins a turbine. As the water flow increases, so does the amount of power that can be produced.

## Sediment and Aquatic Life

Water moves **sediment** as it flows, whether in the path of a river, waves pounding the coast, or floodwaters submerging an area. The greater the flow, the greater the **sediment transport**. Too much sediment can damage ecosystems by burying habitats or ruining the water quality and preventing light penetration. But some sediment is necessary for nest building and the addition of nutrients for plant growth.

EARTH'S HYDROSPHERE

# ACTIVITIES

Chapter three was all about Earth's hydrosphere and how it impacts the planet. You learned about fresh water and salt water, properties of water, frozen water, and how water cycles around Earth. And you traveled both underground to explore aquifers and under the sea to investigate the ocean floor. In this section, there are several hands-on activities for you to enjoy as you apply your newly discovered knowledge.

## Nature Journal

Watch the water cycle at work by observing precipitation such as rain or snow. What does the sky look like? Do you notice any clouds or interesting colors? Consider whether the precipitation is in a solid or liquid state. How big are the drops or flakes? What happens when they hit the ground? Do they infiltrate and sink into the ground, do they pile up, or do they run off? Record your observations in your journal, and be sure to include an illustration to go with your journal entry.

## Water-Cycle Demonstration

You can create a mini water-cycle demonstration in your backyard. You will need a large bowl, a glass jar, a pitcher, water, plastic wrap, string, and a permanent marker. On a warm and sunny day, place your large bowl outside in the sunshine. Put the glass jar in the middle of the bowl, and use a pitcher to add water to your bowl so that the water level is about halfway up around the glass jar (be careful not to get water in the jar). Use a piece of plastic wrap to cover your bowl. You can carefully decorate the plastic wrap "sky" with clouds and a Sun if you would like. Just make sure it is tight around the edges of the bowl. Wrap a piece of string around the bowl if needed to secure the plastic wrap. Observe your setup periodically for a couple of hours, and you should see evidence of evaporation, condensation, and precipitation as the water in the bowl evaporates in the warmth, condenses on the top of the plastic wrap, and "rains" down into the glass jar.

## Surface Tension

It's time to investigate an important property of water known as surface tension. You learned that surface tension is caused by the strong attraction of water molecules to each other. On the surface of the water, the molecules hold on extra tight because the only thing above them is air instead of more water. You can take a walk by a creek or wetland area and look for water striders demonstrating how they take advantage of water's surface tension by moving across the surface without sinking in. You can also test surface tension by using a dropper or pipette, water, and a coin. Slowly add tiny droplets of water to a coin that's lying flat on a table or counter. Guess how many drops the coin will hold before they spill over. Then, count the drops as you add them. Was your hypothesis correct?

## Salinity and Ocean Currents

Visualize the difference in density caused by salinity in the ocean water. You learned about sea ice in this chapter and the importance of ocean currents. As sea ice forms, the water around it becomes saltier, causing it to be denser and to eventually sink beneath the less dense water. This movement can drive ocean currents. For this demonstration, you'll need to gather two glass jars, salt, water, a pipette or straw, and blue and yellow food coloring. Fill up both jars halfway with water. Add about one tablespoon (18 g) of salt to one of the jars, and swirl it around until the salt mixes with the water. Add a few drops of blue food coloring to this jar, and swirl to mix. Add a few drops of yellow food coloring to the jar of water without salt. Fill your pipette (or straw), with some of the blue, salty water. Placing the straw against the inside of the glass jar just above the yellow water line, slowly add the blue water to the jar of yellow water. Carefully observe the stream of blue water as it sinks to the bottom of the yellow water (it will take on a green shade). Look at the jar from a side view, and you'll notice the salty water gathering under the fresh water at the bottom of the jar because it is denser. When salt dissolves in water, it increases the density of the water.

EARTH'S HYDROSPHERE

# ACTIVITIES

## Making Waves

Visit an ocean or lake if possible to observe the waves and movement of water to see how they affect the shoreline. You learned about the power of waves in weathering rock and moving sediment. With this activity, you can create your own waves in a bottle. You'll need a clear plastic water bottle with a lid, water, blue food coloring, and vegetable or baby oil. Fill your bottle halfway with water, and mix in a couple of drops of blue food coloring to make the water blue. Then, fill the bottle the rest of the way with oil. Put on the lid, and turn your bottle on its side. Then, move it back and forth gently to create waves within the bottle. By moving the bottle, you're creating the energy needed to move the water much like the wind does on the ocean or lake surface.

## States of Water

*Adult Supervision Required*

You discovered in this chapter that water on Earth exists in all three states: solid, liquid, and gas. You'll need water for this activity along with a small, clear plastic cup, a dry-erase marker, and a small saucepan to boil the water. Begin by filling the plastic cup halfway with water. Observe the properties of liquid water. Touch it, move it around, and watch how it behaves. Next, set the plastic cup of water on the counter, and mark the level of the water on the outside of the cup with the dry-erase marker. Place the cup in the freezer for several hours to allow the water to become solid. Is the water level still the same? Remember, water is unique in that the molecules actually spread out when in a solid state. How does the water behave when frozen? Does it move around? What does it feel like? Finally, add the solid water (ice) to a small saucepan, and put it on the stove over low heat to melt the ice. Observe the melting process, then turn the heat up slightly to watch the water boil. How long does it take for all the water to evaporate from the pan?

## DIY Water Filter

Make your own water filter to mimic the layers that groundwater travels through under Earth's surface. As water moves through the layers, some of the contaminants may be removed, although the ground doesn't always make the water drinkable. Use a plastic 2-liter bottle, a bowl, scissors, dirt, water, coffee filters, sand, cotton balls, and rocks. Follow the steps to complete the activity.

1. Cut off the top of the plastic bottle where it widens so the bottle is the same width all around. Then, turn the cut-off top over and rest it in the bottom part of the bottle, so it is suspended with space beneath it.
2. Mix up a batch of dirty water in a bowl using dirt and water.
3. Make a filter in the top part of the water bottle by placing a coffee filter in first and then layering rocks, cotton, and sand in whatever order you think would work best.
4. Slowly pour the dirty water over the filter you made, and watch the water come out the opening into the bottom of the bottle. Is the water cleaner?
5. Repeat the experiment using a different order of filter materials. Does the order of filter materials change the cleanliness of the water?

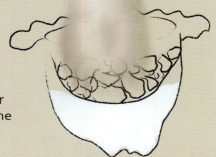

### Did You Know?

Freshwater wetlands help soak up flood waters in their soils while wetland plants and trees help slow flowing floodwaters. Wetlands can reduce the height of flood waters overall and slow erosion.

EARTH'S HYDROSPHERE

# 4

# EARTH'S ATMOSPHERE

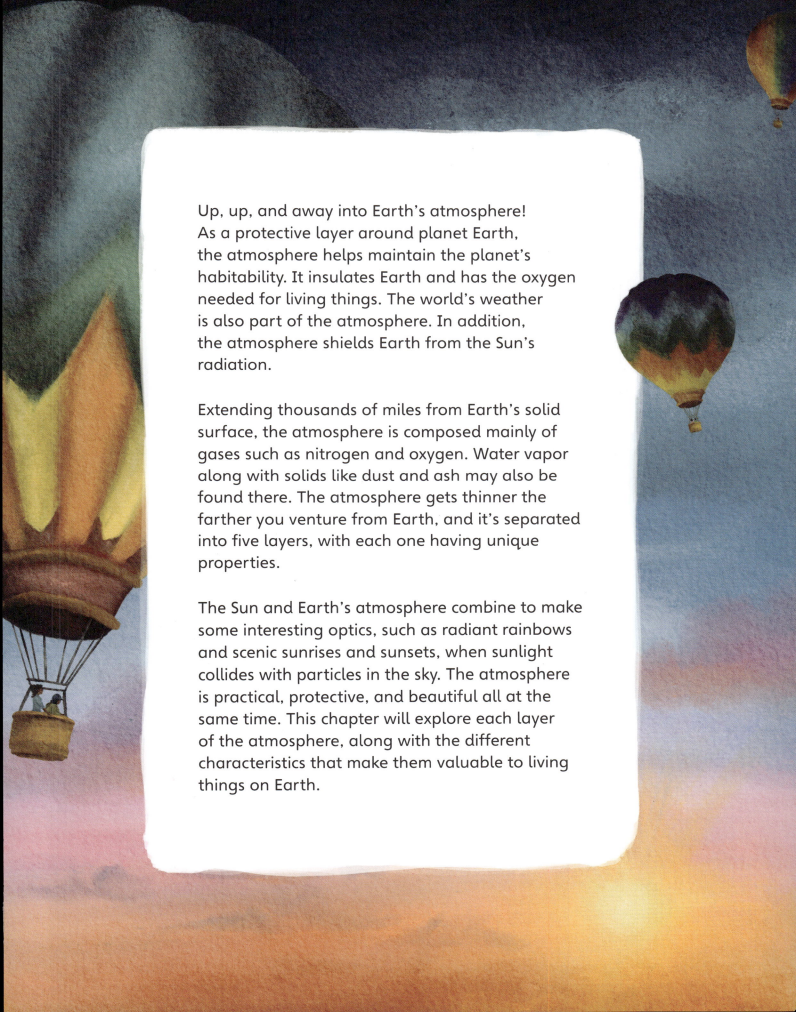

Up, up, and away into Earth's atmosphere! As a protective layer around planet Earth, the atmosphere helps maintain the planet's habitability. It insulates Earth and has the oxygen needed for living things. The world's weather is also part of the atmosphere. In addition, the atmosphere shields Earth from the Sun's radiation.

Extending thousands of miles from Earth's solid surface, the atmosphere is composed mainly of gases such as nitrogen and oxygen. Water vapor along with solids like dust and ash may also be found there. The atmosphere gets thinner the farther you venture from Earth, and it's separated into five layers, with each one having unique properties.

The Sun and Earth's atmosphere combine to make some interesting optics, such as radiant rainbows and scenic sunrises and sunsets, when sunlight collides with particles in the sky. The atmosphere is practical, protective, and beautiful all at the same time. This chapter will explore each layer of the atmosphere, along with the different characteristics that make them valuable to living things on Earth.

# COMPOSITION OF EARTH'S ATMOSPHERE

Reaching 6,200 miles (10,000 km) above Earth's surface, the atmosphere stretches all the way to space, and gravity keeps the atmosphere from floating away. Gases may feel light, but they do put pressure on Earth. They exert the most pressure when they are closest to Earth because gas particles in the air there are much closer together than they are when farther away from Earth's surface. So, higher elevations experience much less air density than those at low levels.

## FUN FACT

Scientists think Earth's early atmosphere may have formed from gases released by volcanoes into the air. Possibly, certain types of bacteria and then plants were helpful in creating and adding oxygen to the atmosphere over time.

NATURE SCHOOL: PLANET EARTH

## Air

Most of Earth's air is found in the first layer of the atmosphere, closest to the planet's surface. Living things need oxygen in the air for respiration and cellular functions. While oxygen makes up 21 percent of the air surrounding Earth, nitrogen is the most common gas in the atmosphere at 78 percent. Argon and carbon dioxide in addition to trace amounts of other gases are also found there.

## Atmospheric Components

The main components of the atmosphere are gases including nitrogen and oxygen. While most of the air around you is formed by gases, also found in the atmosphere are water vapor, water and ice in clouds, and aerosols. Aerosols are solids, such as pollen, dust, and ash, along with pollutants from industrial plants and vehicles.

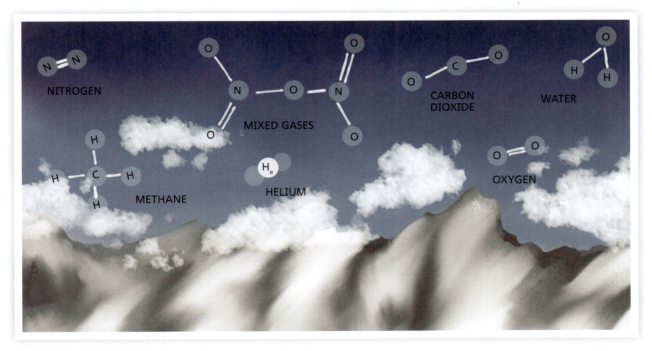

# STRATIFICATION: LAYERS OF THE ATMOSPHERE

With the atmosphere extending over 6,000 miles (9,650 km) from Earth's surface, the air particles in the upper layers are widely spaced, meaning they are much less densely packed than those closer to the ground. Air pressure decreases with elevation as well. Close to the surface, the temperature is usually warmer than at higher elevations, but some of the upper layers have areas where the heat is much greater.

## FUN FACT

The first weather balloons were used in the 1890s to send instruments into the atmosphere to gather information about heights above Earth where people were not able to travel. Thanks to a weather balloon revealing an area of "constant temperature," Teisserenc de Bort, a French physicist, named the stratosphere.

NATURE SCHOOL: PLANET EARTH
88

It's difficult to tell where the **exosphere** stops and outer space starts, as this uppermost layer loses gas particles to outer space because it's so far from Earth's gravitational pull. Some scientists do not consider the exosphere as the upper boundary of the atmosphere, while others say it reaches up to 6,200 miles (10,000 km) above Earth or even farther.

The **thermosphere** is so named because of the temperature increase in this layer due to radiation from the Sun being absorbed. It can get up to 3,600 degrees Fahrenheit (1,980 degrees Celsius) even though it might not feel hot, because the number of gas molecules is so low in the thermosphere. Satellites orbit in this part of the atmosphere, which extends from approximately 53 to 375 miles (85 to 604 km).

From 31 to 53 miles (50 to 85 km) above Earth's surface lies the **mesosphere**. Temperature increases at the bottom of this layer. The gas molecules are thick enough that the mesosphere helps protect the planet from meteor strikes, as meteors burn up traveling through the mesosphere.

The **stratosphere** extends from 11 miles to 31 miles (18 to 50 km) above the planet. It contains almost one-fifth of the gas molecules in the atmosphere, and temperature actually increases with height, with the ozone layer located in the stratosphere trapping heat as it scatters radiation from the Sun.

As the layer closest to Earth, the **troposphere** is the densest. This layer contains the majority of atmospheric gas. Air pressure is highest in this layer, and most weather takes place here. The troposphere reaches higher over the equator than it does at the poles, extending up to 11 miles (18 km) from Earth's surface.

EXOSPHERE
THERMOSPHERE
MESOSPHERE
STRATOSPHERE
TROPOSPHERE

EARTH'S ATMOSPHERE

# THE TRANSFER OF HEAT ENERGY

Energy from the Sun makes life on Earth possible. The Sun's radiation heats the planet to keep water from freezing, and the heat also powers wind and weather. Sunlight provides light, powering photosynthesis, which feeds both humans and animals. In turn, oxygen is produced for respiration.

## Thermal Energy Transfer

Heat energy from the Sun maintains life on Earth. Solar radiation from ultraviolet, visible, and infrared waves both heat and light the planet. Heat causes conduction in Earth's water and land as their particles move around faster and collide, increasing Earth's temperature. Conduction is more common near the ground's surface because particles of solids and liquids are more closely packed. Air nearest to Earth's surface will be heated by conduction. Convection occurs when this warm air rises, and cooler air will sink down to take its place.

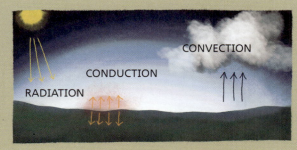

## Earth's Energy Budget

It is important for the amount of radiation from the Sun that reaches Earth and the amount of radiation that goes from Earth into space to be balanced, so the planet does not get too warm or too cool. For example, some sunlight is absorbed by the surface of the planet's land and water as well as the atmosphere. Some radiation is sent into space when it is reflected by the different surfaces on Earth or by the clouds and atmosphere. As Earth absorbs sunlight and heats up, this heat can also be radiated back into space.

### FUN FACT

Solar radiation takes just over 8 minutes to reach Earth from the Sun. Approximately 70 percent of this radiation is absorbed by Earth's atmosphere and surface, and the rest is reflected back into space.

NATURE SCHOOL: PLANET EARTH

# The Greenhouse Effect

The greenhouse effect is a natural way Earth keeps warm and stays livable. Some energy from the Sun that reaches the planet's surface radiates back out as heat. Important greenhouse gas molecules in the atmosphere, such as carbon dioxide and methane, absorb some of that heat, radiating it back to Earth or toward neighboring greenhouse gases in the air. Some of the heat will make it back to space. Burning of fossil fuels and other processes can add greenhouse gases to the atmosphere, which may eventually cause the greenhouse effect to make Earth too warm.

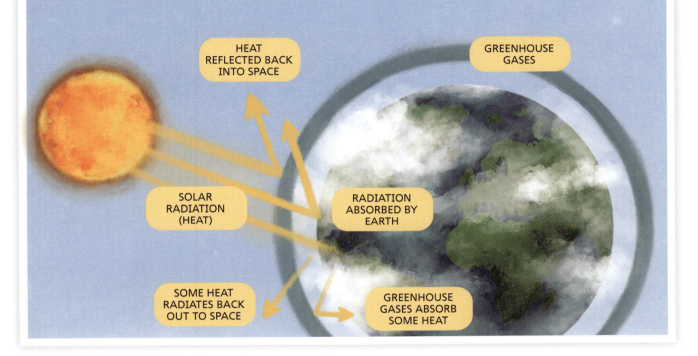

## FUN FACT

Ozone is a combination of three oxygen atoms, and the stratosphere has a layer that contains this marvelous molecule. The ozone layer absorbs damaging ultraviolet radiation from the Sun, providing protection for living organisms on Earth. Certain types of air pollution can damage the ozone layer by making it thinner, impacting its effectiveness.

EARTH'S ATMOSPHERE

# CLIMATE AND WEATHER

Do you live somewhere that experiences changes during all four seasons, or is your weather similar all year long with lots of heat and humidity or dry desert conditions? Climate varies with geographical location due to factors such as topography, elevation, and latitude. While weather represents what the air and atmosphere are like at a particular time of day, the climate in which you live is determined by the average weather over the course of many years. Almost all weather occurs in the troposphere, the layer of the atmosphere closest to Earth's surface. Weather and climate are important for life on Earth because they affect the soil and types of plants that grow in a region, which in turn influences the animals adapted to live there.

## What Causes the Weather?

Weather is influenced by several factors, including temperature, atmospheric pressure, precipitation, clouds, humidity, and wind. Usually, the warmest temperatures occur near the equator, while cooler weather happens near the poles. Atmospheric pressure basically describes the weight of the air overhead. High pressure often leads to clear weather while low pressure is associated with precipitation. Precipitation falls from clouds as rain, snow, sleet, or hail. Clouds are responsible for precipitation and also for shielding the Sun's rays or insulating Earth's surface at night. Humidity is the amount of water vapor in the air. And wind's air movement is based on different temperatures at Earth's surface.

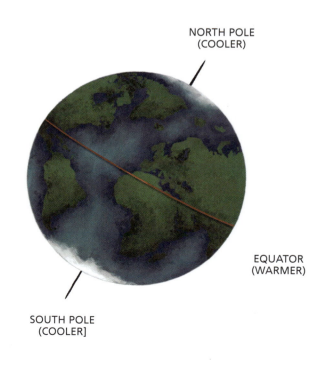

NORTH POLE (COOLER)

EQUATOR (WARMER)

SOUTH POLE (COOLER)

# Weather Systems and Patterns

Movement of low- and high-pressure systems transports air around the world, creating weather patterns. High-pressure systems keep air masses from moving up and condensing to form clouds, so they often bring clear weather. And low-pressure systems are usually accompanied by precipitation. Hot, moist air lifts over the equator because it receives intense sunlight, and the air eventually moves toward the poles. Weather systems tend to move across the midlatitudes, which creates these dynamic weather regions. Across the globe, meteorologists study these factors and more to forecast the weather each day.

### FUN FACT

Absolute humidity is the amount of water vapor in the air, while relative humidity is the amount of water vapor in the air compared to how much water vapor the air can hold at its temperature. The higher the relative humidity, the more "wet" it will feel outside.

EARTH'S ATMOSPHERE

# CLOUDS

Clouds are collections of water droplets or crystals in the atmosphere that are visible because they reflect light from the Sun. They may appear soft and fluffy, dark and foreboding, or flowing and wispy.

## Types of Clouds

There are three basic groups of clouds, and they can vary based on their level in the atmosphere. Knowing the characteristics of the different types of clouds helps meteorologists predict the weather and precipitation in different regions.

- Formed by ice crystals high in the atmosphere, **cirrus clouds** are feathery and are associated with fair weather.
- **Stratus clouds** have layers, as their name implies. They often form when warm air meets a cold front, rises, and cools, so it makes sense they may yield cold rain or snow.
- **Cumulus clouds** are the "typical" fluffy clouds that form when thermals of warm air rise. The name cumulus is from Latin and means "heap."

NATURE SCHOOL: PLANET EARTH

## How Clouds Form

Clouds form when water evaporates from Earth and rises into the air in its gaseous state, called water vapor. As the air rises, it cools, and eventually it's cold enough to condense around dust or other tiny particles, forming droplets. Weather conditions may influence the type of clouds that form in different areas.

## Storm Clouds

When the water droplets in the clouds collect even more water and grow larger, they become heavier and begin to fall toward the ground due to gravity. Rain may be common, but it isn't the only type of precipitation. Rain that freezes while falling is known as sleet. And snow is formed by ice crystals that fall to Earth. Associated with severe weather, hail begins as ice in the cloud when updrafts from strong storms carry water droplets high enough to freeze solid. As part of the water cycle, precipitation is important for watering Earth and the people, plants, and animals that live here.

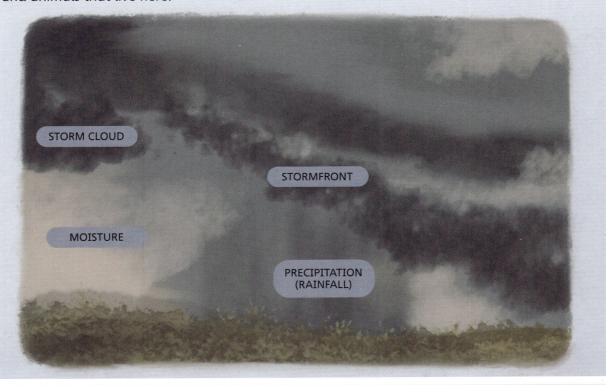

# THE WILD WIND

While you can't see the wind, you can often hear it and definitely feel it. Wind happens when air moves, usually from high-pressure to low-pressure areas. When air is heated near the ground and rises, it lowers the air pressure near the ground, causing wind to blow into that area. The Beaufort Scale is used to measure wind speed from calm to typhoon force. A light wind is known as a breeze, while a gale is a strong, sustained wind. A sudden, strong wind is called a gust.

## Atmospheric Circulation

Prevailing winds blow across Earth's surface in a predictable pattern, usually flowing east and west. These winds come together in convergence zones. Because of their patterned movements, there are several that have been named. One example is trade winds that move from east to west through the tropics. Trade winds are famous for helping explorers throughout history, as they relied on these winds to move their ships quickly across the Atlantic and Pacific Oceans.

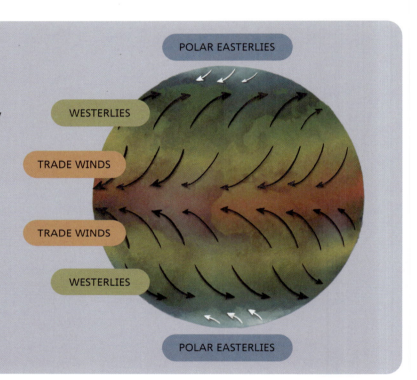

### FUN FACT

Meteorologists use anemometers to measure wind speed and pressure. These devices are located at weather stations around the world, where they can help with daily weather forecasts and predicting changes in weather patterns.

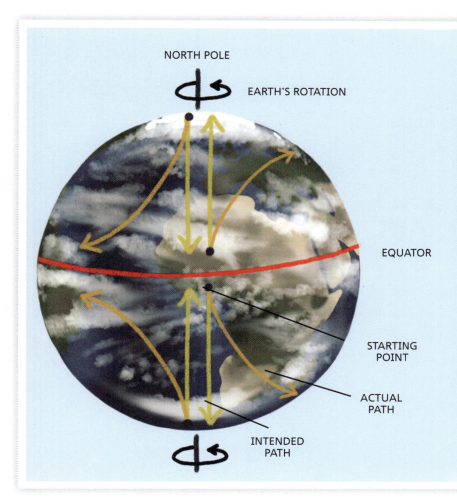

## Coriolis Effect

With warm air rising near the equator and moving toward the poles, the Coriolis effect results in air currents drifting to the right in the Northern Hemisphere and to the left in the Southern Hemisphere. This is due to Earth rotating fastest at the equator and the air moving at a different speed than the ground. Because Earth spins from west to east, the Coriolis force, which is perpendicular, influences north and south movement. These air currents usually start in what's called the "horse latitudes," an area between the equator and 30 degrees north and south.

### FUN FACT

When warm and cold air masses meet, a jet stream of strong winds can form high in the atmosphere. Around the world, there are four major jet streams that flow from west to east—one near each pole and one across each of the subtropical zones.

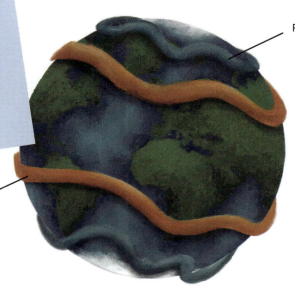

EARTH'S ATMOSPHERE
97

# TYPES OF WEATHER

There are many types of weather because the atmosphere changes regularly due to cloud formations, sunlight reaching planet Earth, and different temperatures of air currents. And weather describes what is happening in the atmosphere at any given time and place. The weather can change from day to day, even hour to hour. From calm to chaotic, weather patterns affect everyone around the world.

## FUN FACT

In the 1800s, the invention of the telegraph was helpful in weather forecasting because it allowed weather observations to be communicated between many geographical regions. Maps of collected data, such as wind and storm systems, were made to study weather patterns.

## RAIN

Water droplets that fall to Earth's surface from clouds in the atmosphere are called rain. Raindrops are usually larger than 0.02 inches (0.05 cm), as smaller droplets are considered drizzle. Rainwater helps refill underground aquifers as well as rivers, lakes, and streams.

## THUNDERSTORMS

Heavy rain along with wind, lightning, and thunder make a thunderstorm. More common in temperate and tropical regions in the spring and summer, they form when hot, humid air rises and brings warmth to the upper atmosphere. Water vapor cools and condenses and forms a cloud high enough to reach freezing temperatures. Colliding ice crystals in the cloud create electrical fields, which can lead to lightning in the clouds or between the clouds and the ground. Lightning strikes cause the surrounding air to heat up rapidly and expand. This expansion is followed by swift cooling and contraction of the air, making a thunderous sound wave.

## SNOW

Water vapor in temperatures below freezing condenses straight into ice instead of liquid, forming ice crystals that keep growing and eventually fall to the ground as snow. Temperature and movement determine the snowflake's shape. Snowfields cover the ground all year long in some areas near the poles and high in the mountains.

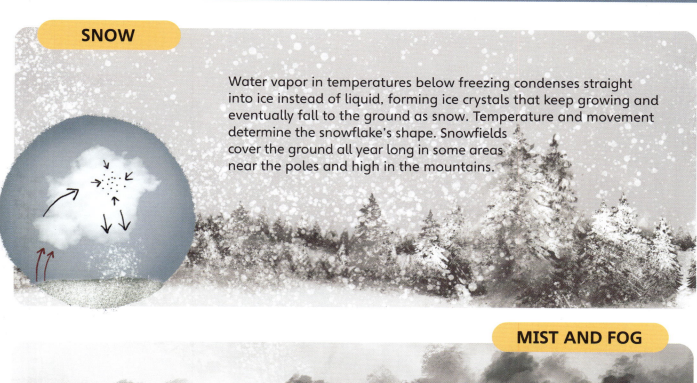

## MIST AND FOG

When clouds touch the ground, we call them fog. Fog reduces visibility because water vapor in the air is condensing near Earth's surface, usually in humid conditions. Mist is also made from water droplets in the air, but mist is less dense than fog. Visibility is usually greater through mist than through fog.

## TORNADO

Tornadoes are dangerous because of their powerful winds! They may form when warm, humid air rises through cooler, drier air. Sometimes in these storms, winds can begin rotating with clouds dropping down in a funnel shape. A tornado is one of these funnels that comes all the way down and touches the ground.

EARTH'S ATMOSPHERE

## HURRICANE

Large storms many miles across, hurricanes form in the warm tropics. While they usually begin in an area of low pressure, as they move over the warm ocean, clouds and thunderstorms form. These storms rotate with the rising warm air and are called hurricanes when their wind speeds reach 74 miles (119 km) per hour.

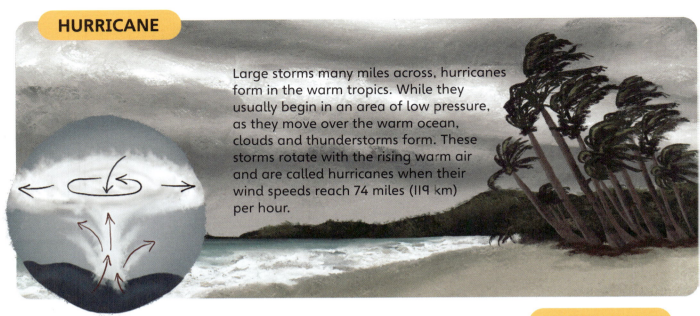

## WATERSPOUT

Sometimes, a rotating column of air will come down from the clouds over a lake or ocean and touch the water's surface. Called a tornadic waterspout, it originates from a severe thunderstorm. Fair-weather waterspouts are more common and are usually short-lived. They form near the surface of the water, rising upward toward cumulus clouds.

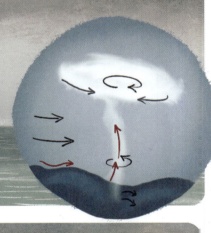

## DUST STORMS AND SANDSTORMS

As wind blasts across the surface of open, flat, and arid regions like deserts, grasslands, and farmlands, it lifts dust and sand into the air. As the storm continues, the clouds increase in size. Sandstorms often don't grow as large as dust storms because sand is heavier.

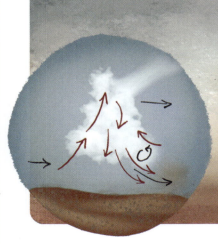

## HAIL AND SLEET

Hail is created high up in a thunderstorm where it's so cold that the water freezes and forms clumps of heavy ice that fall to Earth. Severe thunderstorms may yield hail larger than 1 inch (2.5 cm) in diameter. Sleet is also frozen precipitation but is caused by snowflakes falling through a layer of warm air and partially thawing before refreezing as they pass through a layer of cold air. When they finally reach the ground, they look like little pellets of ice.

## SUNNY

Sunny weather can occur any time of the year when the sky is clear. We usually think of sunny weather as being warm, but it can be sunny in cold seasons, too. High-pressure systems are often associated with clear weather.

## CLOUDY

Cloud cover can impact Earth's temperature and precipitation. Certain types of clouds in a region, such as cirrus or stratus clouds, may mean precipitation is on the way. But clouds don't always cover the whole sky or suggest storms. Low-level cumulus clouds can precede fair weather.

EARTH'S ATMOSPHERE
101

# WHAT WE SEE IN THE SKY

When sunlight reaches Earth's atmosphere, a variety of visual phenomena is created as light is reflected and scattered in interesting and beautiful ways. When light hits particles in the atmosphere such as precipitation, water vapor, gases, and dust, we are able to see things like rainbows, sunrises, sunsets, and halos.

## Auroras

Caused by solar wind bombarding Earth's magnetic field, auroras occur at the poles when some of the charged particles from the Sun enter Earth's atmosphere. When these particles meet with oxygen and nitrogen in the atmosphere, they emit different colors of light, such as red, green, blue, and purple.

## Rainbows

Rainbows appear as an optical illusion when sunlight travels through a water droplet in rain, fog, or other collections of droplets. Sunlight comes into the droplet and is bent or refracted into its different wavelengths before it is reflected back out of the droplet. As sunlight leaves the droplet, it is refracted again. While you usually see an arc-shaped rainbow, they are actually full circles, though you can see only the part above the horizon.

NATURE SCHOOL: PLANET EARTH
102

## Blue Skies

The sky appears blue due to something called Rayleigh scattering. Blue light waves have shorter wavelengths than other colors of visible light, which means they scatter more when sunlight enters our atmosphere and reflects off of particles in the air.

## Colors in the Sky

At sunset, when the Sun is low in the sky, the visible light must travel farther across the atmosphere. The longer-wavelength light waves of reds, oranges, and yellows make it through while the other colors are too scattered. This results in radiant red, orange, and yellow sunsets.

### FUN FACT

When sunlight or moonlight shines through clouds containing ice crystals, you can see halos, spots, or shafts of light form around the Sun or Moon.

EARTH'S ATMOSPHERE
103

# AIR: ESSENTIAL TO LIFE ON EARTH

Without air in the atmosphere, humans, along with other living things, would not survive. Air helps plants and animals make energy for themselves, and air absorbs heat to help keep our planet warm enough for life. Air holds water, which allows clouds to form and precipitation to move water back to the ground. And Earth depends on the air around the planet to shield it from harm.

## Photosynthesis and Breathing

Plants need air for photosynthesis, the process they use to make their own food. During photosynthesis, plants take in carbon dioxide from the air to create food for their cells. From this process, plants make oxygen they release into the atmosphere. Humans and other animals breathe in oxygen, which is added to our bloodstream by our lungs. The oxygen gets carried to the cells all around the body, and cells use oxygen to make energy for them to function.

### FUN FACT

Moving air helps shape Earth by weathering rock and other surfaces and eroding sediment, creating surface features like dunes and wind caves.

NATURE SCHOOL: PLANET EARTH

# Not Just Gas

You know the air contains gases like oxygen, nitrogen, and carbon dioxide, but it also has solid particles called aerosols in it. Aerosols can enter the air naturally through wildfires, volcanic eruptions, soil and rock dust, and salts from the ocean. Humans can also add aerosols to the air through air pollution.

- NITROGEN 78%
- OXYGEN 20%
- MIXED GASES 0.5%
- ARGON 1%
- CARBON DIOXIDE 0.5%

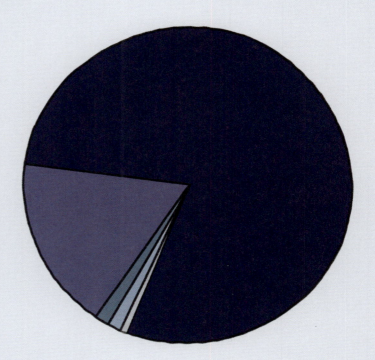

### FUN FACT

Too tiny to see, microorganisms are found in many habitats on Earth, including the air! Miniature bacteria, fungi, and algae called "bioaerosols" are transported by wind and rain. They also fall back to Earth's surface at times, and new ones are picked up from plants, animals, soil, and water.

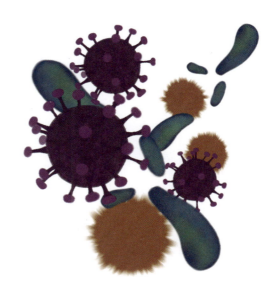

# ACTIVITIES

In this chapter, you learned all about Earth's amazing atmosphere. You discovered the components of air surrounding the planet and how the atmosphere changes as it extends toward space from Earth's surface. You studied how weather patterns form and how the world's weather is influenced by the Sun's energy, the shape of the planet, and air circulation. Now, you are going to do some hands-on activities and demonstrations to experiment with all you've learned about the atmosphere that surrounds Earth.

## Nature Journal

Venture outdoors on any given day, and write your weather observations. Remember, weather includes factors such as wind, temperature, air pressure, sunshine, cloud cover, humidity, and precipitation. You'll want to include all of these in your nature journal entry. You can write a paragraph, a bulleted list, or even a story or poem that includes all these details. And be sure to illustrate your weather observations as well. You can even return to this spot at the same time each day for a week (or longer) to make notes about the weather. At the end of the week, look for patterns or changes in the weather in your notes.

## Greenhouse Effect

Earth has a natural ability to keep itself warm so life can flourish. Earth's atmosphere has carbon dioxide, which works to trap the heat from the Sun, much like the glass roof of a greenhouse. You can create your own example of the greenhouse effect by using two clear glasses, ice, plastic wrap, a rubber band, a cooking thermometer, and a sunny day. Add five ice cubes to each glass. Then, cover one glass with plastic wrap (use the rubber band to keep the plastic tight), and leave the other glass uncovered. Set both glasses outside in the sunlight for 2 hours. After 2 hours, measure the temperature of the water inside the glasses using the cooking thermometer. Which one do you expect to be warmer? Why? Is your hypothesis correct?

## Create a Cloud

*Adult Supervision Required*

You can make a cloud in a jar with just a few items you probably already have at home—a clear glass jar, warm water, a hard-sided ice pack, and a match. Fill the jar one-third full with warm water. Ask an adult to light a match, then blow it out and add it to the jar of water. Then put a hard-sided ice pack over the top of the jar. Observe what happens inside the jar as the water vapor from the warm water travels up to meet the ice pack. The water cools and condenses around the smoke from the match and forms . . . a cloud!

## Assemble an Anemometer

Anemometers are used to measure wind speed, and you can make your own at home using a pencil with an eraser, a dark-colored marker, paper cups, tape, a large pin, straws, and a stopwatch. You will start by taping two straws together. Put one straw over the other one, and tape them together in the middle so they form a plus sign. Tape a cup to the end of each straw, making sure the opening of the cups point in the same direction. Mark one of the cups with the dark marker, making a design you will be able to clearly see as the cups spin in the wind. Finally, push a pin through the spot where the straws overlap and into the pencil eraser to connect the straws (and cups) to the top of the pencil. Your anemometer is ready!

Take it outdoors to measure how fast the cups spin, Count how many revolutions the cups make in 30 seconds by counting each time you see the marked cup go around. You can try it again later to see if the wind speed is the same or whether it has increased or decreased. The more times the cups spin during the 30 seconds, the faster the wind is blowing.

EARTH'S ATMOSPHERE

# ACTIVITIES

## Heat It Up!

Earth's surface absorbs heat from the Sun's radiation. You learned that some colors on Earth, such as light-colored ice, reflect more radiation from the Sun than they absorb, while darker colors absorb radiation and heat up faster. You can test this by taking a piece of black cardstock and a piece of white cardstock and setting them out in the Sun on a flat surface. Put an ice cube in the center of both pieces of paper (make sure the ice cubes are the same size). Which ice cube do you think will melt the quickest? Why? Watch the ice cubes melt, and see if you're correct.

## Rainbows

You usually see sunlight as white light, but it contains all the different colors of light. Light radiates in the form of waves, and each color of visible light has a different wavelength. Red has the longest wavelength, and violet has the shortest. White light can be separated into its different colors when it travels through water droplets in the air. As light hits the droplets, it refracts (bends) because it slows down as it travels through the water. The different colors of light are separated, reflected off the inside of the raindrop, and refracted as the light travels back out again. When the Sun shines through raindrops, a rainbow of colors forms.

You can use a clear glass of water to make your own rainbow. Gather your materials—a clear glass filled halfway with water, white paper, and a flashlight. Balance the glass of water at the edge of a table or counter with a bit of the glass hanging over the edge. Then put the white paper on a chair in front of the glass. Turn on your flashlight, and hold it angled downward behind the glass, shining through the water, so that colors appear on the paper in front of the glass. If you don't have a flashlight, you can try this near a window on a sunny day when light is streaming in. The water in the glass refracts the light from the flashlight, separating the different-colored wavelengths.

NATURE SCHOOL: PLANET EARTH
108

## Frosty Flakes

You learned that precipitation comes from clouds of condensed water vapor in the atmosphere. And snowflake formation depends on the temperature and movement of the flakes as they are created and fall from the sky. In this activity, you are going to catch snowflakes and observe them with a microscope. You'll need black cardstock, a magnifying glass and/or pocket microscope, and warm clothing in which to dress. When you see snow falling, bundle up, and head out with your dark paper and your magnifying glass and/or pocket microscope. The contrast between the paper and snowflakes makes them much easier to view. Hold the paper out to catch the snowflakes. As soon as you have gathered a few, set the paper down on the ground, preferably out of the wind. You could use a porch or garage, anywhere that is cold but slightly sheltered. Don't touch the snowflakes, as they are likely to melt upon contact with your warm hands. Hold your magnifying glass over them. Can you tell what shape they are? If you have a pocket microscope, try using it to look at the snowflakes. What new details do you notice?

## Did You Know?

Earth's neighboring planets have very different atmospheres when compared to Earth! Mars has a much less dense atmosphere of mostly carbon-dioxide gas. Venus has the densest atmosphere of all the rocky planets in the solar system with a much higher percentage of carbon dioxide than Earth's atmosphere has.

# 5

## LIFE ON EARTH

Where there is life, there is the biosphere. Earth's biosphere contains all living things and the areas they inhabit. From microscopic bacteria to monstrous redwood trees, life on Earth remains the only life scientists have found in the universe to date. Biomes across the globe, such as oceans, deserts, forests, and grasslands, teem with plants and animals. These collections of ecosystems include not only communities of living things but also the abiotic, or nonliving, things with which they interact.

The physical parts of ecosystems like the type of soil, amount of moisture, and sunlight determine the plants that grow in an area. As the base of the food chain, plants influence the animals that live among them. Species richness is vital. As plants and animals adapt to fill their niches in communities with many populations of living organisms, biodiversity flourishes.

In order to survive, animals, plants, microorganisms, and even people on planet Earth utilize the natural resources provided by ecosystems. These resources, found in all of Earth's spheres, are closely tied together. The interactions that take place between land, water, air, and the biosphere allow life on planet Earth to thrive.

# BIOSPHERE: EARTH'S GLOBAL ECOSYSTEM

While Earth has many separate forests, deserts, oceans, and grasslands, the planet itself is like one giant, global ecosystem. Each organism living around the world depends on the others as well as the nonliving, natural resources they share, including air, sunlight, soil, water, and more. Every ecosystem may appear to be a separate community, but they all interact on a global scale. Although you only live on a small section of Earth, it is important to remember that your small section is important to the planet as a whole.

### FUN FACT

Scientists estimate there are more than 8 million species of living things on Earth!

## Where Is Earth's Biosphere?

From the soil beneath your feet to the highest treetops and beyond, the biosphere surrounds you. Living things, including you, are part of the biosphere. Environments that house living things are also considered part of the biosphere. So, it makes sense that the biosphere is not confined to one area of Earth, but rather it overlaps the planet's other spheres.

NATURE SCHOOL: PLANET EARTH

# Earth as a System

When viewing planet Earth from outer space, it is not difficult to see how all the spheres operate together as a whole. Some aspects may vary slightly over time, like the amount of plant growth in a region, the populations of predator or prey species, or the levels in different bodies of water, but the planet operates consistently overall. You can think of Earth as the main system with four major parts: land, water, air, and living things.

## Interactions

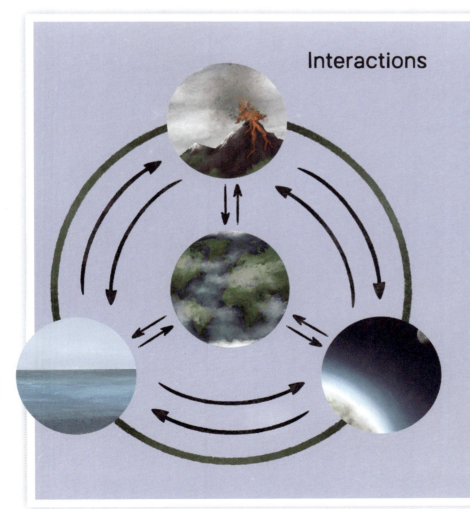

Living things are found in the hydrosphere, atmosphere, and lithosphere, which is why scientists describe Earth's biosphere as overlapping with the other spheres. What takes place in one sphere is sure to impact the others. For example, water that evaporates in the hydrosphere adds moisture to the atmosphere, while water from the hydrosphere impacts terrestrial ecosystems as it sculpts Earth's surface. Animals in the biosphere release carbon dioxide into the air while plants remove this gas from the atmosphere, as well as removing water from the soil.

LIFE ON EARTH

# ECOLOGY: THE INTERCONNECTEDNESS OF LIFE

Ecology is the field of science that studies living things and how they interact with their surroundings, which include both other organisms and nonliving parts of the ecosystem, like soil, sunlight, rocks, air, and water. Ecologists examine ecosystems of all shapes and sizes and in all areas of the world. From microhabitats to biomes, ecology can yield important information about Earth's natural resources.

## Interconnectedness

Since planet Earth is one global ecosystem, it stands to reason that all life on Earth is connected to each other and the nonliving things surrounding them. Plants need sunlight, water, and carbon dioxide to photosynthesize, and most plants also require soil. Microorganisms in the soil help plants get nutrients. Plant seeds are often carried on the wind or by water and can be distributed by animals as well. Animals need water to live in or to drink, and many rely on plants for food and shelter. When even one thing is altered or removed from an ecosystem, everything else is affected.

### FUN FACT

Human ecology is the study of people and their interactions with each other and their surroundings, both natural and human-made.

NATURE SCHOOL: PLANET EARTH

# Levels of Ecological Organization

Within an ecosystem, large or small, collections of living things exist in a hierarchy of organization, from specific to more general groupings.

**Species > Population > Community > Ecosystem > Biosphere**

A single organism represents a **species**.

A group of those organisms in one area is a **population** of that species.

All the populations of different species together in one space make a **community** of living things.

The community of living things, together with all the nonliving things, make an **ecosystem**.

At the highest level, the **biosphere** is the global ecosystem that includes all living things and their interactions.

### FUN FACT

Ecological succession describes the process of ecosystem formation over time, from bare rocks all the way to a thriving community of plants and animals. It begins with the weathering of rocks and hardy pioneer species such as lichens establishing themselves on the rocky areas. These species help continue the weathering process and contribute nutrients as they decompose until more plant species are able to grow there. Eventually, healthy soil will attract a variety of plant and animal species, and the ecosystem will become more stable.

LIFE ON EARTH

# ECOSYSTEMS

Ecosystems of all sizes and complexities must create a community of plants and animals living together and interacting with each other and their physical surroundings. Different types of ecosystems exist around the world and can vary greatly in size, climate, location, terrain, and species. Some examples of ecosystems include different types of forests, coastal and inland wetlands, rivers, oceans, tide pools, estuaries, hot and cold deserts, savannas, prairies, mountains, canyons, and many more. When you look outside your window, what type of ecosystem do you see?

## FUN FACT

Ecosystems can be small, even really small, as long as they contain all the same types of components as a large ecosystem. A rotting log is a great example of a microecosystem supporting plants and fungi as well as animals that hide in the bark and take cover underneath them.

## Biotic and Abiotic

Both **biotic** (living) and **abiotic** (nonliving) factors are important for the success of an ecosystem. Examples of biotic factors include plants, animals, humans, microbes, and fungi. Conversely, things like rocks, sunlight, soil, and water are abiotic but are still necessary for the living parts of the ecosystem to survive.

## FUN FACT

The area where two ecosystems meet and mix together is known as an ecotone. Ecotones have unique properties that may be a combination of the bordering ecosystems or that may be unique to the ecotone. Where mangroves meet freshwater marshes in the southeastern United States, the ecotone is a clear-cut boundary.

NATURE SCHOOL: PLANET EARTH

## Biome

Biomes cover Earth's surface and represent large areas of land with similar climates and similar communities of plant and animal species adapted to the particular region. Biomes span the continents, can be terrestrial or aquatic, and usually include such categories as water, forest, desert, grassland, and tundra. For example, the forest biome includes all areas of the world that are covered in forests. An ecosystem can be just one part of a biome and is defined by the interconnection between the living and nonliving components. Using the forest biome example, a lowland rainforest would be an ecosystem within a forest biome.

## Habitat

Habitats are places in nature where organisms reside. Food, water, shelter, and space are requirements for any habitat. Of course, these requirements vary depending on the size and species of the organisms living there. Habitats are important for each level of organization in an ecosystem, from individual organisms to entire communities.

## Niche

Specific to each species, the niche is the role species play in their ecosystems. Niches exist to allow species to inhabit the same area by utilizing different resources in that area. Some species have a very limited niche while others are generalists.

LIFE ON EARTH

# ECOSYSTEMS AROUND THE WORLD

A variety of ecosystems are found around the world, representing different biomes with similar climates and geography. Aquatic ecosystems are found in Earth's hydrosphere in oceans, lakes, and rivers. Terrestrial ecosystems are spread across the continents and vary greatly, from hot and humid to cold and dry. While scientists know the approximate area of Earth that is covered by oceans, they estimate the land area taken up by various terrestrial ecosystems as shown in the chart below.

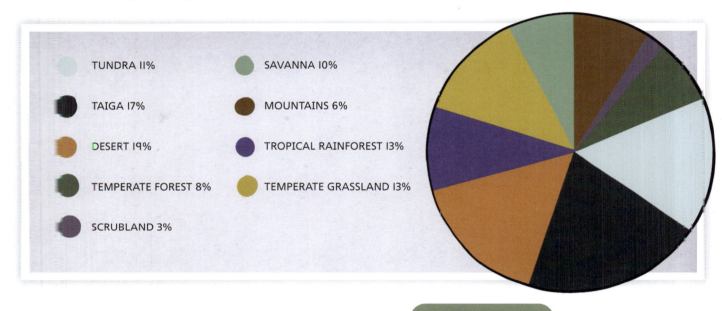

- TUNDRA 11%
- TAIGA 17%
- DESERT 19%
- TEMPERATE FOREST 8%
- SCRUBLAND 3%
- SAVANNA 10%
- MOUNTAINS 6%
- TROPICAL RAINFOREST 13%
- TEMPERATE GRASSLAND 13%

## OCEAN

Oceans are large expanses of salt water that cover a sizable percentage of Earth's surface. Although they are all connected as one world ocean, five different oceans are named based on their location. These include the Pacific, Atlantic, Indian, Arctic, and Southern Oceans. Ocean plants range from microscopic phytoplankton to larger seagrasses and mangroves. Many groups of animals are adapted to ocean life, such as fish, mammals, echinoderms, arthropods, cephalopods, mollusks, and many more! Oceans have abiotic factors, too. These include but are not limited to salt, water, oxygen, sunlight, sand, and other ocean-floor substrates.

## WETLAND

Both freshwater and saltwater wetlands are found around the world. They can exist both inland and along the coasts. Regardless of location, wetlands are areas of land that have standing water for at least part of the year. They can be large, like the Pantanal in South America, or as small as vernal pools that are seasonal from winter into spring. Wetlands have many plant species, like reeds, grasses, and cypress trees. Animals such as amphibians, snakes, birds, and insects use these beneficial ecosystems for food, nesting, and migratory rest areas. Wetlands slow down flood waters, and their plants act as filters.

## FRESH WATER

Freshwater ecosystems include ponds, rivers, lakes, wetlands, and springs. Fresh water is defined as having 1 part per thousand of dissolved salts compared to ocean water, with 35 parts per thousand. Freshwater ecosystems are important to life on Earth, as they supply drinking water for people and animals as well as irrigation for crops that feed much of the world. In addition, as ecosystems, they provide habitats for a variety of aquatic and semiaquatic animals.

## TUNDRA

Tundra ecosystems are found in northern regions of North America, Europe, and Asia and also on mountaintops (alpine tundra). The tundra can get very cold, with average winter lows reaching -30 degrees Fahrenheit (-34 degrees Celsius). This ecosystem is known for open lands with very few trees and very little precipitation. Some soil called permafrost stays frozen beneath the surface. Plants grow low to the ground to avoid winds, lichens are common, and the growing season is usually short. Animals such as mountain goats and marmots may be found in alpine tundra ecosystems. The Arctic tundra supports animals like lemmings, caribou, and wolves.

## MOUNTAIN

Mountains vary greatly in location and climate. They are found on every continent around the world and even in the ocean! Mountains on land host a variety of ecosystems and a large diversity of plants and animals because they can change dramatically with elevation. Depending on the location, deciduous forests might be at the base of the mountain with evergreen forests at higher elevations. Thinner air and colder temperatures near the peak mean fewer plants and animals with adaptations for survival.

## TAIGA

The boreal forest, or taiga, is located between the tundra and the temperate forests in North America, Europe, and Asia. Like the tundra, in the taiga, soil may be partially frozen beneath the surface. Dense stands of conifers such as pines and firs are adapted to the cold temperatures, snow, and nutrient-poor soils. Fungi, mosses, and lichens are more common than small shrubs and herbs in the taiga. Raptors and rodents make their home in this ecosystem, as do moose, lynx, and bears.

## TEMPERATE FOREST

Found in temperate zones around the world, the temperate forest is a dynamic ecosystem because it changes with the seasons. Cold winters, warm springs, hot summers, and cool autumn temperatures mean that plants and animals must be adapted to live in different conditions or find ways to deal with the temperature differences throughout the year. Deciduous trees are common, as are shrubs and herbs. Insects, spiders, reptiles, amphibians, birds, and mammals are commonly found in this ecosystem. Some migrate or hibernate when temperatures plummet, while others are adapted to stay active even in the winter.

## TROPICAL RAINFOREST

Found in warm, humid climates near the equator, tropical rainforests support an abundance of plant and animal life. Dense, leafy tree canopies block much of the sunlight from reaching the forest floor and some of the rainfall as well. Tropical rainforests receive 80 to 400 inches (203 to 1,000 cm) of rain annually, and their temperatures stay hot throughout the year. This ecosystem is among the most biodiverse of any on land, with many of the world's species living among Earth's tropical rainforests.

## GRASSLAND

Windswept prairies of temperate regions, along with savannas in more tropical regions, are grasslands that are dominated by grass species and forbs such as wildflowers. With too little moisture to be a forest and too much to be a desert, grasslands are found on most continents around the world, with Antarctica being the exception. These ecosystems are sometimes taken over for agriculture because they can have rich soils under the ground. Grazing animals are common grassland residents.

## DESERT

Famous for their arid climates, deserts receive little precipitation throughout the year. Plants and animals that call the desert home must be adapted to extremely dry conditions. Usually, desert soil is sandy or rocky with little organic material. Plants that grow in deserts must be able to reach water easily with their roots or store water in some manner. Desert animals often get the water they need from the foods they eat. Some deserts heat up during the day and cool off at night. But not all deserts get warm. Polar deserts, like the ones in Greenland and Antarctica, can be extremely cold, with their water frozen in ice and snow.

LIFE ON EARTH

# LOCATION AND LIFE ON EARTH

What affects climate and influences life on Earth? Location, location, location! Is your weather hot and humid all year long? Do you have lots of snow? Maybe you experience all four seasons over the course of a year. Several factors related to your place on this planet determine its average weather, including temperature, cloud cover, humidity, wind, and precipitation. And all of these are a result of your latitude and longitude.

## Latitude and Longitude

Imagine lines running around Earth from pole to pole and then lines perpendicular to those, running east to west and intersecting the vertical lines. These imaginary lines form a grid system to help pinpoint locations around the world. The most familiar line of latitude, the equator, is measured at 0 degrees latitude, and it divides Earth into the Northern and Southern Hemispheres.

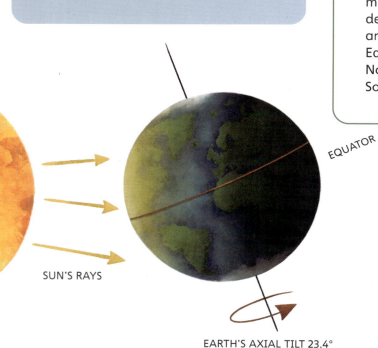

SUN'S RAYS
EQUATOR
EARTH'S AXIAL TILT 23.4°

### FUN FACT

Because of Earth's tilt, the Northern Hemisphere leans toward the Sun part of the year, resulting in summer warmth, while the Southern Hemisphere tilts away during that time and experiences winter. The opposite happens when Earth's orbit results in the Southern Hemisphere pointing toward the Sun.

Locations around the equator receive direct sunlight all year long, so their climates are usually warm. As you move away from this line, increasing in latitude, climates vary more, and temperate climates with seasonal temperature changes occur. The closer you get to the poles, the colder the temperatures are all year long.

NATURE SCHOOL: PLANET EARTH

# Climate Zones

Several climate zones exist around Earth, all having particular characteristics based on their locations. Climate zones may have similar weather as well as comparable ecological communities. Microclimates may exist in each climate zone due to small areas of different conditions caused by natural landforms, bodies of water, and even human-made structures.

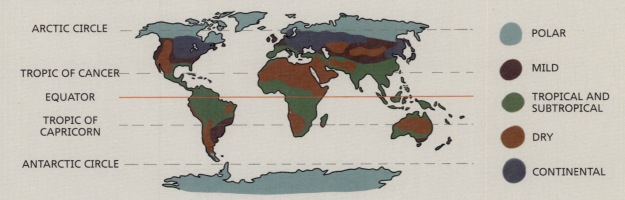

### Dry Climate

- Little precipitation, plus evaporation and transpiration remove water from the environment
- Usually located inland
- May be located near mountains
- From 20 to 35 degrees north and south of the equator

### Tropical and Subtropical Climate

- Warm all year
- From the equator to the Tropics of Cancer and Capricorn
- Often humid, with rain

### Polar Climate

- Cold all year
- May be covered with snow and ice
- Don't receive direct sunlight

### Mild Climate

- Long warm season, short cool season with rain
- Approximately 30 to 50 degrees north and south of the equator
- Often located near coasts of continents

### Continental Climate

- Noticeable changes between seasons
- Warm summers and cold winters with snow
- Inland locations of continents
- Latitudes between mild and polar climate zones

## Life at Elevation

Elevation, or the height above sea level, affects climate as well. As elevation increases in a certain area, temperature usually decreases. This happens despite latitude, so even regions near the equator are cooler the higher you climb.

NIVAL LEVEL

ALPINE LEVEL

MONTANE LEVEL

LOWLAND LAYER

LIFE ON EARTH

# ENERGY FLOW

In any ecosystem, living things need energy to survive. Energy allows cells to function, helps with growth and development, and enables organisms to reproduce. To obtain energy, living things may make their own food, consume other creatures for nutrients, or absorb food from their surroundings. While substances such as water, carbon, and nitrogen may cycle through the ecosystem, energy moves through in a one-way path, flowing from the Sun all the way to the top consumers in the ecosystem's food web.

## Starting with the Sun

The Sun sends energy to Earth through its radiation. Plants absorb sunlight, which helps them to make their own food through the process of photosynthesis. Using sunlight, carbon dioxide from the atmosphere, and water, plants are able to make glucose to power their cells. They also make oxygen during photosynthesis, and plants release excess oxygen through openings on their leaves. This oxygen is used by people and animals all over the world for respiration.

### FUN FACT

The bee and the flower are a type of symbiosis called mutualism, in which both species benefit from the relationship. And it's one you can easily observe. Bees collect pollen from flowers they visit while searching for nectar. In the process, they leave pollen on each subsequent flower they land on, helping pollinate the plants while getting the nectar they need.

## Interactions within an Ecosystem

Species must interact within an ecosystem in order to survive. They may compete with one another for resources, prey upon one another, or even help each other in mutually beneficial relationships. Competition can occur between members of the same species or of different species as they battle over food sources in a small area. Herbivore species feed on plants, and carnivorous animals hunt and eat other creatures. Some species participate in symbiotic relationships with another species where one or both species benefit.

NATURE SCHOOL: PLANET EARTH

# Trophic Levels

In a food web, living things are grouped into trophic levels, sometimes forming a pyramid to show how the energy flows through the ecosystem in which they live. Only a fraction of the energy produced or consumed at each level is available to the animals in the next level because some is lost as heat during cellular functions or as waste products. Energy is highest in the first trophic level, where autotrophs convert sunlight directly into energy that they use. Autotrophs are plants and other organisms that produce their own food, usually through photosynthesis. Consumers, or heterotrophs, have to get their food by eating other organisms. They make up the next levels of the food web. Primary consumers are heterotrophs that eat plants, and secondary consumers eat the animals that eat plants. Tertiary consumers eat the secondary consumers, and this continues on for as many levels as an ecosystem can support. Apex predators are at the top level.

ALGAE (AUTOTROPH) — MUSSEL (PRIMARY CONSUMER) — CRAYFISH (SECONDARY CONSUMER) — RACCOON (TERTIARY CONSUMER) — ALLIGATOR (APEX PREDATOR)

## FUN FACT

Apex predators are the top predators in their ecosystems and have no natural predators themselves. They are important because they keep the ecosystem in balance by helping control prey populations. Some examples of apex predators in their ecosystems are polar bears, saltwater crocodiles, and orcas.

# BIODIVERSITY: THE VARIETY OF LIFE

Planet Earth teems with life from every ecosystem around the world. Biodiversity describes the variety of species living in different regions. The more species present in an ecosystem, the higher the biodiversity is. Terrestrial ecosystems with large numbers of plant species usually exhibit large numbers of animal species as well. So it makes sense that forests are thought to have more biodiversity than other ecosystems on land. Coral reefs are believed to be the most biodiverse ecosystems within the ocean.

## Taxonomy

Taxonomy describes the process of organizing all the world's species into established groups. Scientists give each species a distinct, two-part scientific name to describe and classify them. This international system helps scientists around the world share information about different animals. Scientific classification is organized into a hierarchy of groups called taxa. The highest level is the largest, broadest taxon, and each taxon underneath it is more specific, ending with the species.

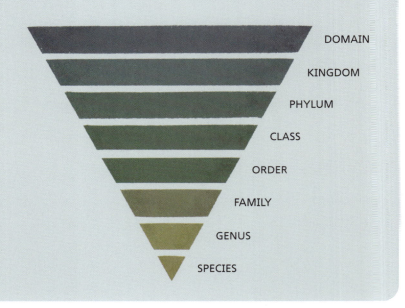

### FUN FACT

Adaptations are physical features or behaviors that help organisms survive in their ecosystems. An example of a physical adaptation is an owl's extraordinary ears, which allow it to hunt in darkness and still catch its prey. A behavioral adaptation used by killdeer involves feigning injury to lure predators away from their nest.

# Domains

Living organisms are divided into one of three domains. Domains are the largest taxa in the classification system and include archaea, bacteria, and eukarya. Archaea and bacteria are usually single-celled organisms and are prokaryotes that do not have a nucleus or complex organelles in their cells. They differ from each other structurally, and archaea are known for their ability to survive in extreme environments. Bacteria are found all over the world! Eukarya differ from archaea and bacteria in that they are more complex and can be single-celled or made of many cells. Plants, animals, fungi, and protists fall under this domain.

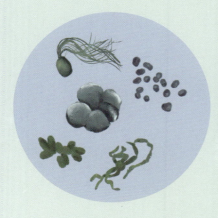  

ARCHAEA　　　　　　　　　BACTERIA　　　　　　　　　EUKARYA

## FUN FACT

An invasive species is one that is not native but that has been introduced to a particular area, whether accidentally or purposefully. Invasive species can sometimes outcompete the native species for resources and lower biodiversity where they have been introduced. Cane toads are an example of a species that is native to Central and South America but that has been introduced to Australia and other countries where they end up poisoning predators that try to feed on them.

LIFE ON EARTH

# LIFE CYCLES

Every organism goes through a life cycle of some kind. Characterized by the sequence of changes organisms display, life cycles explain how living things grow and develop from birth until they are ready to begin the cycle over again. Ultimately, life cycles end when an organism dies. The life-cycle process helps sustain populations of different species within the ecosystem to keep it in balance.

## The Circle of Life

While all living things experience life cycles, not all life cycles look the same. Species are adapted with unique life-cycle processes that work best for them when they have the proper nutrients and environmental conditions available. Take a look at life-cycle examples from these different organisms.

### LIFE CYCLE OF AN AMPHIBIAN

Many amphibians go through metamorphosis, which is a process of changing their body structure from larva to adult. They hatch as tadpoles from eggs, usually in the water, where they use gills to breathe and tails to swim. The larvae eat algae and plants in the water. As they grow, their bodies change, and they develop legs and lungs. Even their diet may change as they begin eating more insects and worms. Adult amphibians often live on land and return to the water to lay eggs and begin the life-cycle process again.

### LIFE CYCLE OF A BIRD

Birds are known for laying eggs in nests. Some chicks hatch from their eggs with feathers covering them, eyes open and ready to move around. They may stay with the mother bird for a while, until they learn how to live on their own. Chicks of other species may be featherless upon hatching, incapable of feeding themselves or moving around. These chicks must stay in the nest and rely on their bird parents to care for them as they grow. Within a few weeks, they are ready to fledge the nest and live on their own. Some species have chicks that display a variation of these different types of development upon hatching.

NATURE SCHOOL: PLANET EARTH

## LIFE CYCLE OF AN INSECT

Insect life cycles differ between species. Some insects do not go through metamorphosis, and they hatch from their egg looking just like the adult, only smaller. Some insects go through a complete metamorphosis with egg, larva, pupa, and adult stages. And there are some in between, like the grasshopper, that experience simple metamorphosis. When grasshopper eggs hatch, the young are called nymphs and look similar to the adult but without wings. Nymphs feed on leaves while they grow bigger and molt approximately five times before emerging in their winged, adult form.

## LIFE CYCLE OF A TREE

Most tree life cycles are similar in that they begin with a seed, such as an oak tree's acorn. With proper conditions like sunlight, water, and space, the seed may germinate and begin to grow. Roots grow down into the soil while shoots sprout upward. Tiny seedlings begin to grow and develop bark and leaves. The seedlings develop into larger, juvenile saplings as they get bigger. Eventually, the tree will mature and be able to develop seeds of its own to begin the process again. Large tree species may take longer to mature than smaller species, and oak trees can take 20 years to produce acorns.

## FUN FACT

Migration involves moving from place to place, often seasonally, and some species migrate in order to reproduce and continue the life-cycle process. Amphibians may travel short distances to get to water where they can lay their eggs. Salmon may leave the ocean to move upriver for breeding, while some populations of giant humpback whales migrate thousands of miles to raise their calves in warm, tropical waters.

LIFE ON EARTH

# BIOCHEMICAL CYCLES

Everything on Earth is made of atoms. While atoms cannot be created or destroyed, they can cycle through the planet and its atmosphere, becoming a part of plants, air, soil, animals, water, or anything made of matter. Atoms that are part of living or nonliving things in the ecosystems that surround them include those found in carbon, nitrogen, phosphorus, and water, among others.

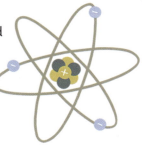

## Carbon Cycle

Carbon is necessary for life on Earth as it provides food energy for living things, helps control the planet's temperature, and allows plants to photosynthesize. Carbon cycles through ecosystems in the plants and animals that live there as well as the soil and atmosphere in their surroundings. Plants take carbon dioxide from the air for photosynthesis, and many animals release carbon dioxide into the atmosphere through their waste and during respiration. Trees and other plants store carbon, and so do soil, rocks, and sediment. Many plants and animals release carbon when they die and decompose. Oceans are also a storage area for carbon, and ocean water exchanges carbon dioxide directly with the atmosphere around it.

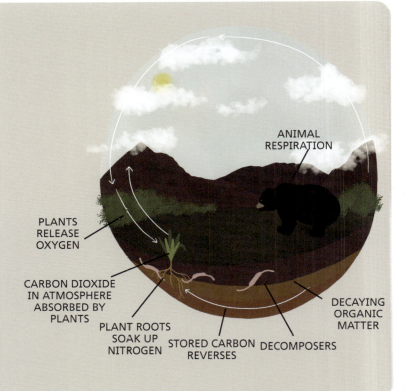

- ANIMAL RESPIRATION
- PLANTS RELEASE OXYGEN
- CARBON DIOXIDE IN ATMOSPHERE ABSORBED BY PLANTS
- PLANT ROOTS SOAK UP NITROGEN
- STORED CARBON REVERSES
- DECOMPOSERS
- DECAYING ORGANIC MATTER

- PLANT & ANIMAL MATTER DECAY
- NEW PLANT GROWTH
- RETURN NUTRIENTS BACK TO THE SOIL

### FUN FACT

As animals and plants die in their ecosystems, decomposers may help return nutrients from these organisms back to the soil to replenish it and allow new plants to grow.

NATURE SCHOOL: PLANET EARTH

## Nitrogen Cycle

As part of amino acids (proteins) and nucleic acids (DNA), nitrogen is important to living things. It cycles through the atmosphere, ground, and water like other important molecules. Nitrogen makes up most of the air in Earth's atmosphere, but microbes in soil, water, and plants play a huge role in "fixing" this nitrogen gas into ammonia for plants to use. Then, animals that consume these plants also consume their usable nitrogen. Some soils have nitrifying microbes that convert ammonia into nitrates for plants to use. Denitrification can occur in the soil as microbes convert nitrates back into nitrogen. As dead plants and animals are decomposed by bacteria, some nitrogen may return to the soil.

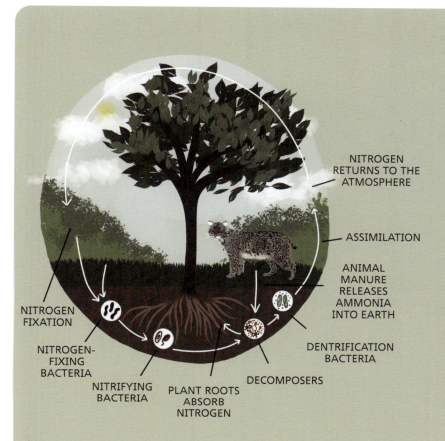

## Water Cycle

The water cycle is necessary for planet Earth to support life, from regulating climate and influencing weather to enabling cellular processes in living organisms. As water flows on and through Earth, its molecules move around the planet. The Sun causes water to heat up and evaporate from Earth's surface and rise up into the atmosphere. As the water travels higher and cools off, it condenses and forms clouds, before precipitation carries it back to Earth. Rain, snow, or other precipitation may soak into the ground or run off into streams, lakes, or other bodies of water.

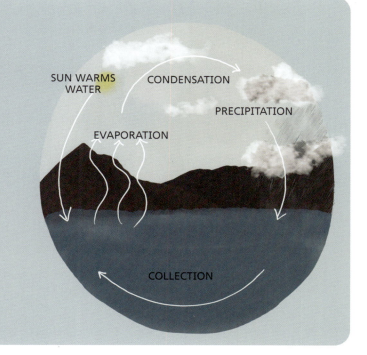

LIFE ON EARTH

# OUR EVER-CHANGING EARTH

Earth abounds with natural resources! Found in every ecosystem around the world, natural resources are things in nature that support living organisms. This broad definition may include factors such as water, soil, land, sunlight, and minerals. These abiotic factors in ecosystems aren't living, but they allow life to flourish. Living things like plants, animals, and fungi are also natural resources. Resources may be considered "renewable" if they can be replenished in a timely manner when properly managed. For example, wood from trees, sunlight, water, and wind are renewable. Nonrenewable resources such as oil and natural gas take much longer to form and cannot be replaced quickly.

## Earth's Natural Resources

**SUNLIGHT**—The Sun provides energy for plants to photosynthesize, and it gives light and heat so living things can survive.

**WATER**—Water allows plants to make their own food, and it carries sediment and helps form Earth's landscape. Animals and other living things use water in their cells, and water helps regulate the planet's climate.

**SOIL**—Soil provides a substrate for things living on Earth and helps filter water. Plants anchor themselves in soil and absorb water and nutrients from it.

**MINERALS**—Minerals are used in building and construction, and some provide vital nutrients to living things. They are useful in technology and industry.

**PLANTS**—Plants are the primary level of food webs in various ecosystems. They provide shelter for animals, and large plants like trees are used in construction. Plants emit oxygen so living things can breathe.

**ANIMALS**—Animals provide food for both predators and humans. They nourish the soil with their waste, and they help to aerate and prepare the soil for new plant growth. Animals act as pollinators and seed dispersers.

**FUNGI**—Fungi act as a food source for animals in many ecosystems. They break down dead organisms and recycle important nutrients through the decomposition process. Fungi live among plant roots to help plants get nutrients from the soil.

NATURE SCHOOL: PLANET EARTH

## Natural Resources in Ecology

As part of an ecosystem, natural resources may be living or nonliving. Because they are necessary for life to exist, they are crucial to planet Earth. Resources may be abundant in some ecosystems and scarce in others. Can you think of an ecosystem where water may be hard to find? Dry deserts may lack water but have plentiful mineral supplies. Do all ecosystems have trees? Forests are filled with trees and often other plants, but grasslands have very few. Wind can be a powerful resource in treeless plains, as can fertile soil. The wise use of resources like these allows them to be conserved for generations to come.

## A Delicate Balance

Earth is a dynamic planet, with ever-changing weather and a land surface that is constantly being transformed. Erosion by wind and water, tectonic-plate movement, and natural events such as earthquakes shape the land surface. Animal and plant populations fluctuate, and water levels rise and fall. But through it all, ecosystems can survive these shifts as their communities adapt and survive. People have the potential to affect each ecosystem's resources positively or negatively, which in turn impacts the entire global ecosystem. Through conservation, it's possible for people to use natural resources while helping the ecosystem stay in balance.

# ACTIVITIES

In chapter five, you examined Earth's biosphere, from the entire global ecosystem to the individual species found within them. You learned about the various living and nonliving factors that interact within ecosystems and the value of the world's natural resources. You studied the way energy flows through an ecosystem from plants all the way to apex predators. Now, complete these activities to review what you've discovered, so you can teach others about the importance of ecosystems.

## Nature Journal

Visit a variety of ecosystems in your region, such as a mountain, prairie, wetland, or desert. Bring your nature journal and a pencil to sketch the entire landscape, or choose one species on which to focus. Make notes about the weather, time of day, and location. Is there an abundance of natural resources? How many different species do you see? How are the ecosystems similar, and how do they differ? Try visiting the same ecosystems at various times of the year. What changes, if any, do you observe?

## Build a Mini Ecosystem

You can build a mini ecosystem in a jar! You'll need a clear jar with a lid, small rocks, soil, a layer of moss collected from the outdoors, and a spray bottle filled with water. Start by adding the rocks to the bottom of your jar, followed by the soil. Spray the soil lightly to dampen it. Then, add the moss on top, pressing down slightly so it's resting on the soil. Give it a couple more sprays of water, then add some tiny figurines or nature decorations. Put the lid on the jar, and set your mini ecosystem in a window so it gets a bit of sunlight during the day. Be sure to observe it daily, and add water or more sunlight as necessary. Enjoy this little slice of nature indoors.

NATURE SCHOOL: PLANET EARTH

## Decomposers at Work

Where can you find decomposers? They are all around, and many are so tiny you can't even see them. Others, such as worms, fungi, millipedes, and larvae, are easier to see. As decomposers recycle nutrients from dead organic matter back into the ecosystem, they help to improve the health of those ecosystems for the species that live there. Look for them in soil and on rotting logs, in compost bins, and even on the forest floor. How many can you find? What do you see them doing?

## Natural Resource Scavenger Hunt

Go for a walk in your neighborhood or in a natural area nearby. Look for the natural resources on the list below. Check them off the list as you find them. Are you able to observe all of them? For an extra challenge, keep track of how many species of each living thing you find or how many types of nonliving things you see.

- Trees
- Grasses
- Flowers
- Animals
    - Vertebrates
    - Invertebrates
- Fungi
- Soil
- Sunlight
- Fresh water
- Salt water
- Rocks

LIFE ON EARTH

# ACTIVITIES

## Classify Your Pet

Using scientists' classification system, classify your pet from its domain all the way to its species. If you don't have a pet, choose one you would like to have. Fill in the following information about the pet of your choice. What other animals are in the same taxa (categories) as your pet?

DOMAIN
KINGDOM
PHYLUM
CLASS
ORDER
FAMILY
GENUS
SPECIES

## Energy Pyramid

Choose your favorite ecosystem, and make an energy pyramid with species found in that ecosystem. You'll need materials to make a 3D pyramid with different colors for each level. You could use salt dough or air-dry clay that you can paint after it dries, Lego blocks, magnetic tiles, etc. You will also need markers to draw species and to label each level or old magazines to cut out pictures (with permission). Remember, the widest layer at the bottom of the pyramid includes producers. Primary consumers then secondary and tertiary consumers follow, with apex predators at the top. After you have constructed your levels, making sure each one is a different color, add pictures or names of living things that fit into the levels, and attach them to your pyramid. When you're all finished, use your model to teach your family and friends about the energy pyramid within your favorite ecosystem.

## Square-Foot Species

Biodiversity refers to the number of different species in an ecosystem, which is important for the health of that ecosystem. A large number of species usually means an ecosystem is healthy. While it would be a challenge to measure the number of species in an entire ecosystem, you can measure a small space within an ecosystem. You'll need a measuring tape or ruler, a pencil, a notebook, four sticks, and some twine. Measure and mark off a square foot (or other square measurement) on the ground in an ecosystem of your choice. With permission from an adult, put one stick in the ground in each corner of your square, then tie the twine around the sticks to mark the square's boundary. Look carefully within your square-foot section for all the different species of living things you can find. Grass, flowers, moss, insects, spiders, fungi—whatever you can see. Make note of them in your notebook by naming or describing them. How many species were in that small section of the ecosystem? Would you describe the biodiversity as high or low? Try the same activity in a different area and compare the results. Why do you think they were similar or different?

### Did You Know?

Species are not always able to adapt to and survive the changes in their ecosystems for various reasons. Sometimes, predators and overhunting can lead to a decline in their populations, as can disease and invasive species. Habitat loss affects species survival as well. When species go extinct, it means there are no longer any living members of that species on Earth.

# ACKNOWLEDGMENTS

### LAUREN

A very special thank-you to my amazing husband for supporting me, to my incredible children for inspiring me, to my parents for believing in me, and to my coauthors, Laura and Stephanie, for making the very best team.

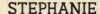

### STEPHANIE

I am deeply grateful to my family for their support and patience. To my friends and coauthors, Laura and Lauren, a heartfelt thank-you for your dedication and hard work on this and all our collaborations.

### LAURA

Special thanks to Lauren and Steph as well as my family, friends, and students for your steadfast support and endless inspiration. Your encouragement means the world to me.

# ABOUT THE AUTHORS

**LAUREN GIORDANO** is an author, illustrator, and owner of Chickie & Roo, an educational curriculum and resource company for families and schools. She home educates her two children in Florida and taught in her local homeschool co-op community, where she led nature classes. Lauren is passionate about bringing children closer to nature and helping them develop a deeper understanding of our natural world. Her work has been featured in The Peaceful Press, A Year of Learning, Chickadees Wooden Toys, Wild + Free Co., FunSchooling Books, and more. You can find her work at chickieandroo.com.

**STEPHANIE HATHAWAY** is a Kansas City–area artist who specializes in creating educational content inspired by our natural world. She believes in using beautiful, dynamic illustrations to make learning about science and nature exciting and accessible to children of all ages. She is guided by the notion that many of life's valuable lessons can be learned from nature. It is her hope that her work will inspire families to explore and learn from the natural world right outside their own door. You can see more of Stephanie's educational nature-based studies and original artwork at stephaniehathawaydesigns.com.

**LAURA STROUP** is the founder of Firefly Nature School, a nature study curriculum designed for homeschooling families, co-ops, and classrooms found online at fireflynatureschool.com. Laura has a bachelor of science degree in animal ecology from Iowa State University with an emphasis in natural resource education. A former museum educator and upper school science teacher, she now directs School of the Wild, an immersive nature school that serves her local community. Laura resides in the countryside near Springfield, Missouri, with her family.

# INDEX

**A**

absolute humidity, 93
abyssal plains, 70
abyssopelagic zone, 71
activities
  anemometer, 107
  biodiversity, 137
  centrifugal force, 58
  cloud creation, 107
  cyanotypes, 33
  decomposers, 135
  Earth layers, 56
  Earth model, 56
  Earth topography, 56
  ecosystem jar, 134
  energy pyramid, 136
  film canister rocket, 35
  fossils, 59
  greenhouse effect, 106
  groundwater filtration, 83
  journaling, 32, 56, 80, 106, 134
  night hiking, 34
  night-sky painting, 34
  ocean currents, 81
  ocean salinity, 81
  pet classifications, 136
  planetary exploration, 32
  plate tectonics, 58
  rainbows, 108
  rock painting, 57
  rotation of Earth, 58
  salinity, 81
  scavenger hunt, 135
  sediment jar, 59
  snowflake observation, 109
  solar radiation, 108
  solar system model, 32
  square-foot biodiversity, 137
  surface tension, 81
  volcano, 57
  water-cycle demonstration, 80
  water filter, 83
  water states, 82
  waves, 82
adhesion, 67
aerosols, 87, 105
air, 86, 97
air pressure, 86, 88, 89, 93
albedo, 76, 77

ammonia, 131
amphibians, 119, 120, 128, 129
anemometers, 96, 107
animals
  abyssopelagic zone, 71
  adaptations, 126
  apex predators, 125, 136
  bathypelagic zone, 71
  birds, 119, 120, 128
  carbon dioxide from, 113
  competition, 124
  decomposition, 130, 131
  epipelagic zone, 71
  fossils, 59
  hadalpelagic zone, 71
  heterotrophs, 125
  hibernation, 11, 120
  invasive species, 127
  life cycles, 128
  lotic ecosystems, 73
  migration, 11, 119, 120, 129
  ocean animals, 118
  primary consumers, 125, 136
  respiration, 124
  symbiotic relationships, 124
  taxonomy, 126
  temperate forests, 120
  tertiary consumers, 125, 136
  trophic levels, 125
  tropical rainforests, 121
  tundra, 119
  water and, 95
  wetlands, 119
Antarctic ice sheet, 77
apex predators, 125, 136
aquatic ecosystems, 118
aquifers, 65, 75, 79, 90, 98
archaea, 127
Arctic Ocean, 68, 118
argon, 87
Aristotle, 39
Armstrong, Neil, 31
asteroids, 17, 24, 25, 62
asthenosphere, 39, 42
astronauts, 30, 31
astronomy, 30
astronomical units (AU), 35
Atlantic Ocean, 68, 69, 96, 118
atmosphere. *See also* weather

aerosols, 87, 105
air, 87, 97
air pressure, 86, 88, 89, 93, 96
auroras, 102
carbon and, 109, 130
cirrus clouds, 94
clouds, 92, 94–95, 98, 107, 131
components of, 87
conduction, 90
convection, 90
Coriolis force, 97
cumulus clouds, 94
currents, 97
exosphere, 89
formation of, 86
greenhouse effect, 91, 106
halos and, 103
horse latitudes, 97
jet stream, 97
Mars, 109
mesosphere, 89
ozone layer, 91
pollution, 87, 91, 105
rainbows, 102, 108
Rayleigh scattering, 103
size of, 85, 86, 88, 89
sky color, 103
stratosphere, 89
stratus clouds, 94
sunsets, 103
temperatures, 88
thermosphere, 89
troposphere, 89, 92
Venus, 109
water cycle and, 95, 131
winds, 96
atoms, 12, 66, 130
auroras, 102
autotrophs, 125

**B**

bacteria, 45, 105, 127, 131
beaches, 50, 53, 61, 79
Beaufort Scale, 96
bioaerosols, 105
biodiversity, 69, 113, 126, 137
biomes, 117
biosphere, 111, 112, 113, 115
birds, 119, 120, 128

NATURE SCHOOL: PLANET EARTH
140

black dwarf stars, 29
black holes, 13
Bort, Teisserenc de, 88
brackish water, 73

## C
canyons, 52
carbon, 26, 27, 28, 76, 124, 130
carbon dioxide, 53, 87, 91, 104, 109, 113, 114, 124
caves, 53
Ceres, 17
chalky soil, 45
Chicxulub crater, 25
chromosphere, 16
cinder cone volcanoes, 49
cirrus clouds, 94
classification system, 136
clay soil, 45
cliffs, 55
climate zones, 123
clouds, 92, 94–95, 98, 107, 131
cohesion, 67
comets, 24
conservation, 133
constellations, 39
continental crust, 42
continental margin, 70
continental rise, 70
continental shelf, 43, 70
convergent boundaries, 47
coral reefs, 126
Coriolis effect, 40, 69, 97
corona, 16
cosmonauts, 31
crust, 37
cryosphere, 63, 76
cumulus clouds, 94
cyanotypes, 33

## D
decomposers, 130, 135
deltas, 73
denitrification, 131
deserts, 53, 100, 121
diurnal cycle, 21
divergent boundaries, 47
domains, 127
dust storms, 100
dwarf planet, 17

## E
Earth
  aphelion, 20
  asteroid impacts, 24, 25
  axis, 20
  centrifugal force, 41, 59
  core, 37, 38, 40
  crust, 37, 38, 39, 42, 44, 56
  diameter, 38
  distance from Sun, 20, 35
  formation, 28
  gravity, 28, 41, 58
  Gutenberg discontinuity, 39
  inner core, 38, 56
  location, 17
  magnetic field, 16, 39, 40, 41, 102
  magnetosphere, 16, 27, 40, 41
  mantle, 36, 37, 38, 39, 42, 46, 48, 56
  Moon and, 22
  name origin, 62
  orbit, 14, 15, 18, 20, 24
  outer core, 37, 38, 39, 56
  perihelion, 20
  plates, 39, 46, 47, 50, 58
  shape, 38, 39
  size, 18
  Sun and, 16, 20, 21
  tilt, 24, 122
earthquakes, 38, 46, 47, 48, 133
eclipses, 13, 23, 39
ecology, 114–115
ecosystems
  abiotic factors, 116, 118, 132
  adaptations and, 126
  biodiversity, 69, 113, 126, 137
  biomes, 117
  biotic factors, 116, 118
  carbon cycle, 130
  conservation, 133
  deserts, 121
  domains, 127
  ecological succession, 115
  ecotone, 116
  energy flow, 124–125
  food webs, 125
  grasslands, 121
  habitats, 117, 137
  hierarchies, 115
  interconnection, 114
  microecosystems, 116
  mountains, 120
  natural resources, 132, 133
  niches, 117
  nonrenewable resources, 132
  ocean ecosystems, 118
  renewable resources, 132
  sizes of, 116
  taiga, 120
  temperate forests, 120
  terrestrial ecosystems, 118, 126
  tropical rainforests, 121
  tundra, 119
  variety of, 116, 118
  water cycle, 131
  wetlands, 119
electricity, 39, 40, 67, 79, 98
electrons, 12, 66
epipelagic zone, 71
equator, 20, 38, 59, 68, 89, 92, 93, 97, 121, 122, 123
erosion, 43, 48, 55, 59, 78, 79, 133
eukarya, 127
eutrophic lakes, 72
exosphere, 89

## F
fish, 71, 118
flooding, 79, 83, 90, 119
floodplains, 73
fluvial processes, 50
fog, 99
food webs, 124, 125, 132
fossil fuels, 91
fossils, 45, 59
free ions, 67
freshwater, 63, 65, 68, 72–73, 77, 81, 83, 116, 119
fungi, 45, 105, 116, 120, 127, 132, 135, 137

## G
Gagarin, Yuri, 31
galaxies, 13, 14, 15, 31
Galilei, Galileo, 30
geologic time scale, 29
geomagnetic storms, 41
glaciers, 44, 50, 52, 54, 55, 63, 65, 72, 73, 77
globular clusters, 15
goldilocks zone, 26–27
grasslands, 121
gravity
  atmosphere and, 86, 89
  black holes, 13
  Earth and, 28, 41, 58
  globular clusters, 15
  gravitational pull, 13, 15, 16, 22, 23, 24
  Moon and, 23
  rain and, 95
  star formation and, 29
greenhouse effect, 91, 106
groundwater, 63, 74, 75, 77, 79, 83, 90
Gulf Stream, 69
Gutenberg discontinuity, 39

INDEX
141

## H
habitability, 26, 27, 85
habitat loss, 137
hadalpelagic zone, 71
hail, 92, 95, 101
heliopause, 17
heliosphere, 13
helium, 16, 29
Hera (Greek goddess), 15
heterotrophs, 125
hibernation, 11, 120
hills, 55
hillslopes, 50
horse latitudes, 97
Hubble Space Telescope, 30
humidity, 92, 93, 106, 122
hurricanes, 100
hydrogen, 16, 29, 62, 66, 67
hydrosphere, 62, 113, 118

## I
ice, 17, 24, 62, 65, 67, 76, 77, 87, 101, 103
igneous processes, 50
igneous rocks, 43
impermeable rock, 74, 75
Indian Ocean, 68, 118
insects, 119, 120, 124, 128, 129, 137
intergalactic space, 13
International Space Station (ISS), 31
interstellar space, 13, 17
invasive species, 127, 137
iron, 18, 28, 37, 39
islands, 49, 50, 54

## J
jet stream, 97
Jovian planets, 17
Jupiter, 17, 19, 24, 30, 35

## K
Kuiper Belt, 17, 19
Kuroshio Current, 69

## L
lakes, 27, 50, 63, 64, 65, 67, 72, 73, 77, 82, 100, 119, 131
latitude, 39, 77, 97, 122, 123
lava dome volcanoes, 49
lithosphere, 39, 42, 46, 47, 113
loam, 45
longitude, 122
lotic ecosystems, 73
lunar eclipse, 23, 39

## M
magma, 42, 43, 47, 49, 52, 70
magnetic field, 16, 39, 40, 41, 102
magnetosphere, 16, 27, 40, 41
mantle, 37, 38, 39, 42, 46, 48, 56
Mariana Trench, 68, 71
marine life, 70, 71, 118, 125, 126, 129
marine processes, 50
marine snow, 71
Mars, 17, 18, 27, 35, 62, 109
Mercury, 17, 18, 35
mesopelagic zone, 71
mesosphere, 89
mesotrophic lakes, 72
Mesozoic Era, 25, 29
metamorphic rocks, 43
metamorphosis, 128, 129
Meteor Crater, 24
meteorologists, 93, 94, 96
meteors, 24, 25, 89
methane, 19, 91
microecosystems, 116
microorganisms, 44, 45, 105, 114
Midnight Sun, 21
mid-ocean ridges, 70
migration, 11, 119, 120, 129
Milky Way, 11, 14, 15
mist, 99
molecules, 66, 67, 81, 82, 89, 91, 131
Moon
　Earth and, 22
　eclipses, 23
　far side, 22
　gravitational pull, 23
　halos, 103
　illumination of, 22, 103
　landings, 31
　light from, 34
　lunar eclipse, 23, 39
　near side, 22
　observation, 9, 13, 30, 34
　synchronous rotation, 22
　tides and, 23
mountains, 39, 47, 48, 49, 50, 51, 52, 53, 55, 70, 77, 99, 116, 119, 120
mutualism, 124

## N
natural resources, 114, 132, 133, 134, 135
Neptune, 17, 19, 35
neutrons, 12
niches, 111, 117
nitrogen, 26, 27, 79, 85, 87, 90, 102, 105, 124, 130, 131
nonrenewable resources, 132

## O
observable universe, 12
oceans. *See also* water
　abyssal plains, 70
　animals, 118
　Arctic Ocean, 68, 118
　Atlantic Ocean, 68, 69, 96, 118
　bathypelagic zone, 71
　biodiversity, 69
　brackish water, 73
　carbon storage, 130
　Challenger Deep, 71
　continental margin, 70
　depth, 68, 71
　epipelagic zone, 71
　Indian Ocean, 68, 118
　life in, 70, 71, 118, 126, 129
　Mariana Trench, 71
　mesopelagic zone, 71
　mid-ocean ridges, 70
　oceanic crust, 39, 42, 70
　Pacific Ocean, 48, 68, 69, 96, 18
　ridges, 47
　salinity, 68, 81
　seas compared to, 68
　Southern Ocean, 68, 118
　submarine vehicles, 71
　tides, 22, 23
　volcanoes, 70
oligotrophic lakes, 72
Orion Spur, 15
outer core, 37
outer solar system, 17
oxygen, 62, 66, 67, 87, 90, 102, 104, 124
ozone, 91

## P
Pacific Ocean, 48, 68, 69, 96, 118
peat, 45
pedosphere, 44
perched water table, 74
permafrost, 76, 77, 119
phosphorus, 79, 90, 130
photosynthesis, 26, 27, 63, 70, 71, 90, 104, 114, 124, 125, 130, 132
phreatic zone, 74
plains, 54
planetesimals, 28
plants
　atmospheric formation and, 87
　autotrophs, 125
　carbon and, 130
　decomposition, 130, 131
　fossils, 59
　invasive species, 127

life cycles, 129
lotic ecosystems, 73
mesopelagic zone, 71
mutualism, 124
ocean plants, 118
photosynthesis, 26, 27, 63, 70, 71, 90, 104, 114, 124, 125, 130, 132
pollination, 124, 132
ponds, 72
sediment and, 79
temperate forests, 120
trophic levels, 125
tropical rainforests, 121
tundra, 119
water and, 63, 75, 95
wetlands, 83, 119
plasma, 16
plateaus, 54
plate tectonics, 46, 58
Pluto, 19, 62
polar deserts, 121
pollination, 124, 132
pollution, 64, 87, 91, 105
ponds, 72, 119
precipitation. *See* hail; rain; sleet; snow
prevailing winds, 96
primary consumers, 125, 136
prokaryotes, 127
protons, 12
proton stars, 29

### R
radiation, 26, 41, 108
radioactivity, 38
rain, 44, 64, 73, 74, 75, 79, 80, 90, 92, 94, 95, 98, 102, 105, 108, 121, 131
rainbows, 102, 108
Rayleigh scattering, 103
red giant stars, 29
renewable resources, 132
reptiles, 119, 128, 129
rift valleys, 47
Ring of Fire, 48
rivers, 27, 48, 50, 52, 55, 63, 64, 65, 73, 79, 98, 116, 119
rovers, 27

### S
salinity, 68, 81
sandstorms, 100
sandy soil, 45
saturated zone, 74
Saturn, 17, 19, 24, 35
sedimentary rocks, 43
sedimentation, 48

seismic waves, 48
shield volcanoes, 49
shooting stars, 25
silt, 45
sleet, 92, 95, 101
snow, 57, 64, 65, 71, 73, 74, 75, 76, 77, 79, 80, 90, 92, 94, 95, 99, 101, 109, 120, 121, 122, 123, 131
soil, 44, 45, 48, 65, 79
solar nebula, 29
solar prominence, 16
solar system, 14, 17, 31, 32
solar wind, 16, 27
Southern Ocean, 68, 118
spring water, 74, 75
stars, 15, 26, 29
stellar halo, 15
stratosphere, 89
stratovolcanoes, 49
stratus clouds, 94
subduction zones, 47
submarine vehicles, 71
subsurface water, 62
Sun
  albedo, 77
  auroras and, 102
  autotrophs and, 125
  chromosphere, 16
  corona, 16
  cyanotype activity, 33
  distance to Earth, 35
  Earth and, 16, 20, 21
  eclipses, 13
  formation of, 29
  geomagnetic storms, 41
  gravitational pull, 16
  halos, 103
  heliosphere, 13
  ice and, 76
  life and, 90
  life span, 29
  location, 15
  lunar eclipse and, 23
  magnetosphere, 16
  midnight Sun, 21
  photosynthesis and, 26, 27, 124
  planetary orbits, 30
  radiation, 16, 90, 108, 124
  size, 16
  solar prominence, 16
  solar winds, 16
  sunsets, 103
  temperature, 16
  water cycle and, 131
  as yellow dwarf star, 29
surface tension, 81

### T
taiga, 120
taxonomy, 126
tectonic processes, 50
telescopes, 30
temperate forests, 120
terrestrial ecosystems, 118, 126
terrestrial planets, 28
tertiary consumers, 125, 136
thermosphere, 89
thunderstorms, 98
tides, 22, 23
topography, 51
tornadoes, 99
trade winds, 96
transform boundaries, 47
tropical rainforests, 121
troposphere, 89, 92
tundra, 76, 117, 118, 119, 120
Tunguska event, 25

### U
Uranus, 17, 19, 35

### V
valleys, 50, 55, 73
Venus, 17, 18, 30, 35, 109
volcanoes, 38, 46, 49, 57, 70

### W
water. *See also* oceans
  as abiotic factor, 116
  absolute humidity, 93
  adhesion, 67
  aquatic ecosystems, 118
  aquifers, 65, 75, 79, 90, 98
  biodiversity, 69
  brackish water, 73
  chemical symbol, 67
  cohesion, 67
  condensation, 64
  conductivity of, 67
  cryosphere, 76
  currents, 69
  cycle, 64–65
  density, 66
  drinking water, 74, 119
  epipelagic zone, 71
  erosion, 78, 79
  eutrophic lakes, 72
  evaporation, 64, 65, 67, 68
  flooding, 73, 79, 83, 90, 119
  floodplains, 73
  fog, 99
  formation, 61, 62
  forms, 64, 65, 66, 67, 72

free ions, 67
freshwater, 63, 65, 68, 72–73, 77, 81, 83, 116, 119
glaciers, 44, 50, 52, 54, 55, 63, 65, 72, 73, 77
groundwater, 63, 74, 75, 77, 79, 83, 90
hail, 92, 95, 101
humidity, 92, 93, 106, 122
hydraulic action, 78
ice, 17, 24, 62, 65, 67, 76, 77, 87, 101, 103
lakes, 27, 50, 63, 64, 65, 67, 72, 73, 77, 82, 100, 119, 131
marine snow, 71
mesotrophic lakes, 72
molecules, 66, 67
oligotrophic lakes, 72
perched water table, 74
permafrost, 77
phreatic zone, 74
plants and, 63, 75, 95
ponds, 72, 119
rain, 44, 64, 73, 74, 75, 79, 80, 90, 92, 94, 95, 98, 102, 105, 108, 121, 131
reservoirs, 65, 79
rivers, 27, 48, 50, 52, 55, 63, 64, 65, 73, 79, 98, 116, 119
saturated zone, 74
sediment, 79
sleet, 92, 95, 101
snow, 57, 64, 65, 71, 73, 74, 75, 76, 77, 79, 80, 90, 92, 94, 95, 99, 101, 109, 120, 121, 122, 123, 131
soil moisture, 75
solar system and, 62
spring water, 74, 75
storage, 64, 65, 66
storm surges, 79
subsurface water, 62
surface tension, 63, 67, 81
water cycle, 80, 131
waterspouts, 100
water table, 74
water vapor, 67, 95
waves, 53, 55, 78, 79, 82
wetlands, 65, 83, 119
weather. See also atmosphere
  absolute humidity, 93
  Beaufort Scale, 96
  clear weather, 101
  climate compared to, 92
  clouds, 92, 93, 95, 98, 101
  Coriolis effect, 97
  dust storms, 100
  elevation and, 123
  Equator and, 92
  flooding, 73, 79, 83, 90, 119
  hurricanes, 100
  influential factors, 92
  latitude and, 122
  location and, 92
  longitude and, 122
  meteorologists, 96
  mist, 99
  poles and, 92
  prevailing winds, 96
  rain, 44, 64, 73, 74, 75, 79, 80, 90, 92, 94, 95, 98, 102, 105, 108, 121, 131
  rainbows, 102, 108
  sandstorms, 100
  sleet, 92, 95, 101
  snow, 57, 64, 65, 71, 73, 74, 75, 76, 77, 79, 80, 90, 92, 94, 95, 99, 101, 109, 120, 121, 122, 123, 131
  thunderstorms, 41, 98, 100, 101
  tornadoes, 99
  trade winds, 96
  weather balloons, 88
weathering, 43, 44, 50, 78, 104
wetlands, 65, 72, 81, 83, 116, 119
white dwarf stars, 29
winds, 69, 92, 96

## Y

yellow dwarf stars, 29